Mexican Genealogy Research Online

A Guide to Help You Discover Your Ancestry

2nd Edition

Mexican Genealogy Research Online

A Guide to Help You Discover Your Ancestry

2nd Edition

Moises Garza

Mexican Genealogy Research Online

A Guide to Help You Discover Your Ancestry

Published by Moises Garza

Copyright © 2014 Moises Garza.

ISBN-13: 978-1502941046

ISBN-10: 150294104X

This book was printed in the United States of America

DEDICATION

I want to dedicate this work to my wife Clarissa Perez and my two sons, Matthew Jacob Garza and Marcus Jayden Garza.

Also to my parents Lauro Garza Marroquin and San Juana Tanguma Lopez, without them I would not even be here. Their wedding picture is on the front cover of this book.

Finally, to all my ancestors whom the sands of time have buried and I will never be able to find.

CONTENTS

ACKNOWLEDGMENTS

I owe special thanks to my wife Clarissa, for all her support and encouragement in writing this book.

To all the MexicanGenalogy.info readers whom requested this book, and most importantly, for their continued readership and support.

Before you Begin Reading This Book

The reason that the first edition of this book did not get printed and was only available as an eBook was that it contained hundreds of links. Some links of those links where over thirty characters each, thus making it difficult for the reader to access those resources. To change that what I have done for this printed edition is add short links besides each link.

Text that is underlined in this book is an actual link on the digital eBook. In this book after each underlined text I have added a short link. This short link will appear inside parenthesis, you can enter this short link into your browser in order be taken to that particular resource.

Example of original link:

http://www.familytreemagazine.com/upload/images/PDF/ancestor.pdf

Short Link:

(http://mexgenlink.com/z5m7)

In this example both addresses will take you to the same resource. The original link is hard to type on a browser and if it changes there is no way of changing it in this book. On the other hand, the short link is easy to type and can be updated even if the original link changes thus always keeping this book current.

I did not include short links to resources that are easy to type, for example; google.com, familysearch.org, etc... The benefits of short links is also immense, they not only help you get to the resource you want but it also helps me keep all links up to date thus, making this book relevant even if the original link for that resource changes.

Another thing to keep in mind, this book contains many links to resources on the internet. Please keep in mind that nothing on the internet is set in stone, and some resources may cease to exist while others are moved to other websites, or the links may just simply be changed. If you find that a short link is not working, please send me an email to moisesgarza@gmail.com and I will promptly fix it.

Now that we got this very important point out of the way let's get started.

Getting Started with Your Mexican Ancestry Online Research

I want to congratulate you on your interest to find your Ancestry. It is a journey that is very rewarding and fulfilling. As you do your research I know you will come across obscure history and events. In your findings you will learn that your ancestors also played a role in the shaping of two countries and how our lives are solely the product of those men and women that came before us.

Getting Started in Mexican Genealogy online research is very simple and easy, that is if you already have experience. If you don't, don't worry this book will show you how to get started. In the long run it will also save you countless hours that you would have had wasted trying to learn by yourself. Once you are done reading this book you will have a solid foundation to start researching and looking for your ancestors.

As you read this book make sure to pay close attention to the chapter titled "Your Family is the Place to Start", since this is your starting point and there is no way around it. Your family can save you a lot of time and effort in finding your ancestors. Place close attention to the clues they provide. If possible, record your interviews or at the least make sure to write notes since you might quickly forget most of what you heard.

I want you to keep an open mind and adapt my examples to make them your own, think of ways that you can use the resources that I present to you in your own research.

Now that you have decided to look for your ancestors it is time to get started by having a mentality shift. In the next section you will read about common misconceptions that I had and many other people have about Mexican genealogical research. Let's begin.

Five Common Misconceptions about Mexican Genealogy Research

Have you ever wanted to start looking for your Mexican Ancestors only to find yourself discouraged with misconceptions about Mexican Records and or Research? When I started genealogy back in 1998 I had various misconceptions myself about Mexican Genealogy Research. It is my purpose or hope that I will help you get rid of those misconceptions that you may have, holding you back.

Misconception # 1: I live in the Unites States and It Will Be Impossible to do Mexican Genealogy Since I don't go to Mexico

Many people believe, just as I did, that it was impossible to do Mexican Genealogical Research from the Unites States. In reality you can do most research by just using a computer and networking with other researchers in the U.S. and in Mexico. I know this since I have done it myself. Thanks to FamilySearch.org most Church Records and Civil Records before the 1930's are available online.

Misconception # 2: Mexico Has No Records Online

This is true and at the same time false. It is true since the Mexican Government hardly has any records online. But false since FamilySearch.org has almost all Civil Registry Records starting since its implementation in 1859. FamilySearch also contains most Church Records since the early 1500's to the 1950's and in some cases present times.

Misconception # 3: There Are No Books about My Ancestors

Boy oh boy was I wrong, I have found books with stories greater than life, about Indian fighters, Royal Lines, Soldiers, Generals, Conquistadores, and Explorers. One of my ancestors even wrote about the History of one of the provinces of New Spain. The key is to look for rare books. Also there are many great places online to find books and I will talk about them later in this book.

Misconception # 4: My Ancestors Were Poor and Doubt They Left Wills

To date I have found many wills, they are transcribed or short excerpts from the originals. Most of them, since my ancestors were from Northeastern Mexico, are in the Archives of Monterrey. I found them with the help of several books that had indexed those archives. These wills offer a window into the lives of our ancestors.

My Family is Not Catholic, I Doubt My Ancestors Were Catholic

I had the same misconception when it came to my own family. When I started asking questions I was very surprised to find out that only me and two other brothers of mine were not baptized in a Catholic Church. Turns out that my parents were raised Catholic and then became New Born Christians. History will also show us that almost everyone in Mexico Pre 1900's was Catholic. It was a way of life and it was also the only religion most people had contact with. I'll bet you anything that your Mexican Ancestors were Catholic and their records can be found in the Church Records available for Mexico.

The above misconceptions may not be the same as yours but what I want you to do is for you to change or get rid of anything that may be holding you back.

Now that I have provided you with a glimpse of the possibilities, let's get started. In the following section I talk about the most important place to start researching and that is with you family.

Your Family Is the Place to Start

If you are reading this it means that you have decided to start your own family Genealogy quest and most likely you just started to research your family. This quest is very rewarding and fulfilling and once you begin it can be very addicting. I have been doing my own genealogy research since 1998 and it all started with a piece of paper that my grandmother handed to my father which contained the names of her grandparents. Unfortunately she had no other clues of whom her great grandparents where, and or where they came from.

Before I dive any further let me explain something. When I first started I would only collect names, dates, and stories and believed it was OK. Unfortunately, if your credibility ever comes into question it is very important to always know where you got that name or that date. This will also help you while doing your research in case you ever need to re-verify your information. So the first advice I will give you and probably the most valuable and important is to always cite your sources. Sourcing your information, is basically documenting where you got your information. Yes it is extra work and most of the time not enjoyable but this way you will always know where your information came from and believe me sometimes when I review my sources and go back I always find new clues that lead to greater discoveries.

If you don't know how to properly cite your sources don't worry about it, just make sure to jot down names, places, and dates while doing interviews of family members. Also write the names of books and page numbers and always copy URLS for internet sources. Remember the goal is to always be able to find the information if you ever need to. For more help on properly citing your sources, check this out PA Style (http://mexgenlink.com/q2xr) or MLA Style, (http://mexgenlink.com/6trq) both of these links will help you immensely on citations. (Next section explains why it is very important to do so).

Hopefully you will hear my advice and avoid many headaches in the future. OK, now to the fun stuff. The first thing is first, you need to create your family tree starting with yourself and if researching your wife's/husband's family, start their tree with them. Download and print this Five Generation Ancestor Chart (http://mexgenlink.com/z5m7) to help you out and keep things a bit more clear. Once again start with yourself.

Fill in as much information as possible. You will quickly find out that there is a lot missing and a lot that you do not know or cannot remember but don't worry, for right now just focus on you and your wife/husband.

Once you cannot continue any further by yourself it is time to call or email your relatives. Start with your parents. I recommend you get a notebook to jot notes down specially names, dates, and stories. Remember anything can be a clue to find documents in the future. Once your parents cannot remember any further details, if they are still alive, talk to your grandparents. Don't forget to write who you interviewed and the date since that is your citation.

Hint - Ask for pictures or documents and scan them. They will be more inclined to let you scan them than to part with them. I usually carry my laptop and a portable scanner.

You can use the following PDF document Family Group Sheet Form (http://mexgenlink.com/egxd) to do family groups. You can use it to write down all the siblings of your grandparents. In case you need to figure out how you are related to other people here is also a Relationship Chart (http://mexgenlink.com/mtks) to help you decipher these relationships while doing research.

I prefer making interviews by phone since it is easier than traveling especially if they live in another state. I know that I said you don't have to leave your home, but some family will only be comfortable talking face to face.

You can also interview you uncles, cousins, and even your grandparent's brothers or sisters. Think out of the box on whom you can interview and I do suggest you interview everyone that you can think of specially the older generation of your family. Believe me at first you will feel nervous and jittery but it is ok. After several interviews you will find out that your family is very approachable and that they love talking about their families.

Now that you know where to get started and you have the basic charts to start your family tree, let's focus more on citation and why they are so important.

Genealogical Evidence, Is your Ancestor Really Your Ancestor?

I hope that as you continue or start searching for your Mexican Ancestors that you do document every person that you add to your family tree. As I mentioned before when I started, I was just a name collector. That is right a "Name Collector" that is what genealogist call people whose only focus is collecting names. That was several years ago, and my family tree used to have close to 20,000 names.

My information would come from books, internet, and other peoples family trees. I was ok with this and if you are a name collector that is fine with me but if you are ever asked to prove why you claim an ancestor to be yours, how will you prove it?

This happened to me. I was asked about a particular ancestor and could not prove that he was my ancestor. Up until that point I had no citations or notes of where I had gotten my information from. It was that day that I decided to restart my family tree and not add anyone to my tree without a citation or original document. I started with myself and then worked my way back. Now days I can trace many of my ancestors back to the 1500's and can even provide copies of original documents to prove my ancestry.

If at this point you are not citing your sources and or trying to obtain documents I highly recommend that you start doing it. Your research will take new life. You will also find more information about your ancestors than just dates and places.

To help you learn a bit more I have included a link to a PDF document that Rosalinda M. Ruiz prepared about Genealogical Evidence. She does a great job of explaining it.

View or Download PDF Document:

The following is the link to this PDF document by Rosalinda.

- Genealogical Evidence – By Rosalinda M. Ruiz (http://mexgenlink.com/enzm)

Don't be scared about citing your information, you will be thankful later when you revisit a particular ancestor and you are able to retrace your steps as to why you decided to add them to your tree.

Here are some resources about citing:

These are two other great resources to help you do citations.

- APA Style (http://mexgenlink.com/7ge5) – This is the one I have used since college.
- MLA Formatting and Styling Guide (http://mexgenlink.com/l68t)

Even if you do not use the above mentioned formats just make sure to include; the name of the author, name of book or website, internet address, and or anything that will help readers or whomever locate the source where you obtained your information.

So far you have been using paper and pen to write down your family's information. Also writing citations is difficult especially if you are using a pedigree chart or a family group chart to build your family tree. In the following section I will introduce you to genealogy software that will help you create, manage, and cite your family tree.

Genealogy Software to Manage Your Family Tree

So you have gathered as much information that could possibly be gathered from your family and have organized it. If you attempted to organize it that is fine since you have probably noticed that the family charts and forms are kind of hard to follow and organize. At this point that is where Software that has been made especially for genealogy comes into place. Here I will recommend to you only software that I have used and can provide you with honest information. Later on you can explore other ones that will better fit your needs.

The first thing that you need to know is that most software follows the Gedcom standard or at least try to follow it. This is the format that all your data is saved as and makes it easier to change or upgrade software; it is also used to back up your data. Just be aware that if you change from one program to another there will always, if not most of the time, be errors since some programs go above and beyond Gedcom standards and collect extra information that other programs do not support.

The two software programs that I have used extensively are Family Tree Maker from Ancestry.com and Family Tree Builder from myheritage.com. The first one is sold for $39.00 and the second is free, but additional features require a subscription. See the following short reviews of each and my recommendations as to which one I recommend for you to use.

My Favorite Two

Family Tree Maker

This one is my favorite since it lets you back up your family tree online for no additional cost and has superb citation capabilities. The timeline is great and it also has a map to easily see all the locations your ancestors lived at. It lets you also keep track of your research and has tools to help you analyze your data. It also has many reporting features to show case your family tree and ancestry provides an app for your tablet or cell phone. **Price:** $39.00 Visit Website (http://familytreemaker.com)

Family Tree Builder

This software is free to download and install all you need to do is register with a valid email address. They let you upload a 250 person tree to the web for free and anything beyond that you need to start paying a subscription fee. But to use this software on your computer there is no limit as to how many people you can enter. It also lets you print reports and charts, but it does not have a good research tracker or very good citation capabilities. If you are in a tight budget I recommend it since you will not find anything better out there that is free. They also have an app for your tablet or cell phone. Visit Website (http://www.myheritage.com) / Download Now (http://mexgenlink.com/qz1i)

As far as I can see both of these are great programs and have great features and in my opinion they are the best. I have tried others but they did not work for me.

My recommendation is if you can afford it, to go with Family Tree Maker since it has better capabilities for citations and lets you keep better track of your research by letting you create tasks. Also the backing up to the internet and their android app are great. But if you are short in cash and don't want to spend a dime go with Family Tree Builder just be aware that the citation capabilities are not as powerful and you can only back up family trees of less than 250 persons to the internet. They also have an android app which I never tested, but I have heard people say they like it. I used their free software for over seven years and still use them since their software will let you know of any matches on other online trees.

Try them both and see which one you prefer. The important thing here is for you to choose one and start entering the information that you have already collected. Remember don't enter any information that you don't have proof for and if you do decide to enter it, make notes indicating that more research is needed to verify information and why you added it.

Whichever software you use make sure to also enter all your pictures and scanned documents.

Now that you are aware of software to manage your family tree and documents, I am going to tell you about websites where you can also manage your family tree online.

Five Websites to Help You Manage Your Family Tree Online

I know that at this point you may be anxious to start researching your ancestors but first let's talk about having your family tree online. This will also help you have a second copy of your tree on a safe place. Having your family tree online will also let you share it with your family and friends, whom can be a great resource and allies in your research.

As I mentioned before, there are many programs to help you manage your Ancestors Family Tree and some of them even sync to the cloud.

The ones that I have used that do sync to the cloud are Family Tree Maker and MyHeritage, but I do know that there are many others.

Reasons You May Consider to Have a Family Tree Online

- Backup - In case your computer dies.

- Collaborate - You can always invite other family members to help you out.

- Connect With Distant Relatives - You will discover and or get discovered by distant relatives thus providing you with an opportunity to find photos, and stories about your ancestors.

- Share the wealth - Yes, you may have the clue that someone else may need to find their common ancestors with you.

These reasons are the ones that have compelled me into having my own family tree online.

What Websites Can You Use?

The following websites are just some that will let you make a family tree online, a tree that you can share with your friends and family.

They are all free but on some of them additional features may cost you some money.

- ancestry.com - "Is the world's largest online resource for family history with more than 2.5 million paying subscribers across all family history sites."

- myheritage.com – "Our vision has been to make it easier for people around the world to use the power of the Internet to discover their heritage and strengthen their bonds with family and friends."

- wikytree.com - "Is a collaborative community of genealogists and their family members growing a 100% free worldwide family tree."

- geni.com - "Geni is the world's leading collaborative genealogy site. Our world family tree contains more than 69,708,476 connected profiles."

- FamilySearch.org - "Connect Generations, discover your place in history with Family Tree, an easy way to preserve your genealogy online. See what others have contributed, and share your family story."

As I stated before there are other websites that you can use to make and share your online family tree. The above mentioned are just a few that you can get your feet wet with. NOTE: If you have entered all your family on your software you can just export a Gedcom and upload it to any of the above websites. You do not have to recreate your family tree online manually, that would be crazy.

What I Personally Use

I personally use and prefer Ancestry.com since all the information I enter on my computer syncs effortlessly with my online tree and then it syncs to my android tablet and cell phone. The only cost that I have done with Ancestry is buying their software for my PC. Having your Family Tree online with them is free and their android app is also free.

I also use them since sending invitations to family members and friends is easy and straight forward. All you do is send them an email through Ancestry.com and you are done. Once they get this invite in their email they will be able to see your family tree.

The Future

FamilySearch Trees holds great promise and is rapidly becoming the main online family tree website for many people. At least half if not all of the records that you find online will come from FamilySearch and the ability to link them to you family tree is great. I do plan on using them but will do the jump once I feel that I am ready. For now I am just testing them out.

Which one should you Use?

I recommend that you try them all and use the one that you feel the most comfortable with and or the one that satisfies all your needs when it comes to your genealogical research.

At this point you already have the tools to manage your family tree. Hopefully by now you have also found at least five generations of your family by filling out the pedigree chart. I will now tell you in the next section about Google Search. Google Search is one of the best resources to finding your ancestors. After time you will agree with me.

Using the Power of Google Search to Find Your Ancestors

I know that when you think about your ancestors you do not think about Google Search (https://www.google.com). I hope that the following paragraphs change that, next time you want to discover an ancestor I want you to automatically think about Google and it's various search capabilities.

In recent years Google has become a powerful resource especially for genealogist and hobbyists alike. More than 70 percent of all internet users search Google and it is also the place where millions if not billions of websites are indexed.

I have found hundreds of ancestors by just using Google. You might be thinking "yeah right Google".

From my own experience I have come out to find hundreds of websites and family histories that have been indexed by Google. Thus when you search for an ancestors name it is very likely that you will find them. If you are lucky you will also find stories, documents, and of how your ancestor's lives intertwined with history.

Let me also give you a word of caution, if your ancestor does not show up in Google don't assume that there is no information about him or her. Also use the information you find with caution since it might also be incorrect. What I do is just use it as clues to find original documents or copies of original documents.

Here are the two most helpful tips to use when using Google to help you find your ancestors. Remember you enter these techniques in Google's Search Box.

To Find Exact Phrase matches Use Quotes

- "Moises Garza" - This will only return results with Moises Garza.

- "Moises Garza Tanguma" - This will only return results containing Moises Garza Tanguma.

Go ahead give it a try; enter the names of your great grandparents without using quotes and note the number of results. Now try the same names using quotes and see the difference. This will sort out a lot of insignificant results. For example when you do this you get exact results and not all results for Garza or Moises or Tanguma. Thus, this narrows down the search for your ancestors.

Searching a Single Site

Let's say you find a website but it has no search bar, but you need to see if your ancestor is listed. The following tip will help you find them fast.

- site:raullongoria.net francisco rodriguez

You first enter site:followed by a website address and then your ancestors name. The above example shows me searching Raul Longoria's website for Francisco Rodriguez. This technique will work for all websites and it is very useful. In the next section I elaborate more on this technique.

Also, please be aware that these techniques are more successful when searching for ancestors five to six generations or further back since most of the time someone has already done the research and has posted it online.

When you search for more recent Generations Google will most of the time only return obituaries, obituaries are an awesome source of genealogical information. I will elaborate more on this on another section.

Other More Advanced Google Search Options

- For more advanced options you can visit Google Search Operators (http://mexgenlink.com/906h). I have yet to use these methods but I know that they might be useful to you.

Ancestor Search Using Google Custom Search

Randy Majors has developed a very useful tool to search Google for ancestors and I have used it many times. It simplifies the search entries and you don't have to remember to enter any special characters as quotes.

- This great tool is available at his website randymajors.com

Remember that Google is and will become one of your most powerful tools to finding your ancestors online. Make sure and learn how to use it properly. I briefly touched on how to search websites in this section and I will go more in depth on this subject in the next section.

Find Your Ancestors by Learning Proper Ways to Search a Website or Blog

Learning how to search a blog or web site is very important since this can be the difference between finding and not finding your Ancestors.

How to Conduct a Search on a Blog or Website

The first thing to do is locate the search bar. It will usually be to your right hand side or on the header part of the blog or website.

Then just enter your phrase and press enter on your keyboard or the button that says "search".

Once you do this the blog will start searching for all keywords entered and provide you with all the blog posts or pages where they appear.

To narrow down your search you can use quotes, this will let the blog know that you only want search results that are exact match phrases.

Whichever method you use you can always use CNTRL+F (if using windows) or CMD+F (if using a mac) to locate your keywords among all the results.

When you press enter, your browser should highlight all the instances of your search term.

What If There Is No Search Bar On The Website or Blog?

I know that you will run into this problem very often. The way around this is by using Google to search the entire website or blog for your desired keywords.

To do this all you need to do is open up Google.com and on the search bar type;

site: followed by the website domain name and desired keyword to search for.

Example:

site:wearecousins.info garza

As you can see you need to type **site:** to let Google know that you only want to search that particular website or blog. Then you enter the domain name next to site: with no spaces. Then press the space bar and type the keyword that you are looking for.

Remember you can also use quotes to narrow down the search results.

Your Spelling May Be the Key to Finding Your Ancestors

When searching any blog or website you might also want to keep in mind that you need to search for different spellings of names and last names. You might also want to try misspelling variations.

For example:

Lopez & Lopes, Gonzalez & Gonzales, and jose & joseph

Make sure and try many variations since let's not forget that people including us are not perfect, especially when writing.

You might also want to see the following PDF, <u>Spanish Name Abbreviations</u> (http://mexgenlink.com/jnic), for more examples.

A guide to Internet Searches

For more on how to do internet searches, check out <u>FamilySearch's Searching Guide</u> (http://mexgenlink.com/uzo9).

Don't go any further in this book until you have at least used the technics explained here twice. Repetition will only make this a second hand nature.

After you have learned this, it will be time for you to move on to the next section where I show you why it is very important to know your history.

Do You Know Mexico's History? Specially, Local History Where Your Ancestors Came From

I have come to realize that in order for me and you to be able to conduct better research into our ancestors past it is very important to educate ourselves in the history of Mexico, especially on the history of the area that they were from.

I have come cross people and also online family trees that claim that their ancestor was born on a certain date and on a certain town but it does not make sense since that town was founded 30 to 40 years later. They assume that, since their ancestor died in that town he must have been born there also. This is a totally wrong assumption.

Some time back I came across someone asking for help in finding their ancestors church birth record in Camargo, Tamaulipas, Mexico. This person told me that his ancestor was born there in about 1726. From the get go I knew that he was wrong. After probing a bit he told me that he was assuming. I asked if he knew the local area's history and he said no. I proceeded to educate him a bit. I advised that

Camargo was not founded until March 5, 1749 and that most of the founding families came from Cerralvo, Cadereyta, Monterrey, and the surrounding towns. In my own case all my ancestors from Camargo where originally from Cerralvo. I also advised that no church was there before that date and that they should look into the records of Cerralvo and Cadereyta, turned out that their ancestor was from Cadereyta.

As you can see from this example it is always good to get to know the area's history since it will lead you in the right direction. A simple wikipedia search for Camargo would have provided him with this page: http://en.wikipedia.org/wiki/Camargo_Municipality,_Tamaulipas (http://mexgenlink.com/njr7) which contains what I told them.

A couple of minutes of reading can make a big difference.

The following links will let you get familiar with Mexican History since I think it is important to research Mexico's history all the way from its colonial period to present days. This will help you understand your ancestors better and also give you a taste of what events your ancestors lived through. It can also provide you with clues as to the migration patterns that your ancestors might have had taken.

Mexican History Links

- Timeline of Mexican history (http://mexgenlink.com/750n) – Quick and to the point timeline of Mexican history events.
- History of Mexico (http://mexgenlink.com/bu58) – More comprehensive and detailed history of Mexico.
- Territorial evolution of Mexico (http://mexgenlink.com/zsf5) – Very interesting article on Mexican territory.

- <u>Administrative divisions of Mexico</u> (http://mexgenlink.com/xebn) – Provides you with history about Mexican States.

Mexican State Links

The following links will take you straight to their Wikipedia pages. Also please note that each state page has a link to all its municipalities and that is how you get to the very local history of where your ancestors might have been from.

- <u>Aguascalientes</u> (http://mexgenlink.com/na0g)
- <u>Baja California</u> (http://mexgenlink.com/7fzq)
- <u>Baja California Sur</u> (http://mexgenlink.com/uviy)
- <u>Campeche</u> (http://mexgenlink.com/lhfw)
- <u>Chiapas</u> (http://mexgenlink.com/f4p6)
- <u>Chihuahua</u> (http://mexgenlink.com/9p7j)
- <u>Coahuila</u> (http://mexgenlink.com/9zpr)
- <u>Colima</u> (http://mexgenlink.com/jcqu)
- <u>Durango</u> (http://mexgenlink.com/kdlf)
- <u>Guanajuato</u> (http://mexgenlink.com/j13p)
- <u>Guerrero</u> (http://mexgenlink.com/y0i3)
- <u>Hidalgo</u> (http://mexgenlink.com/9vrb)
- <u>Jalisco</u> (http://mexgenlink.com/8top)
- <u>México</u> (http://mexgenlink.com/72mo)
- <u>Michoacán</u> (http://mexgenlink.com/fpnu)
- <u>Morelos</u> (http://mexgenlink.com/um1e)
- <u>Nayarit</u> (http://mexgenlink.com/fj0t)
- <u>Nuevo León</u> (http://mexgenlink.com/plek)
- <u>Oaxaca</u> (http://mexgenlink.com/4hya)
- <u>Puebla</u> (http://mexgenlink.com/sk07)

- Querétaro (http://mexgenlink.com/ak4j)
- Quintana Roo (http://mexgenlink.com/if8o)
- San Luis Potosí (http://mexgenlink.com/39rn)
- Sinaloa (http://mexgenlink.com/0t34)
- Sonora (http://mexgenlink.com/8tpp)
- Tabasco (http://mexgenlink.com/ybb6)
- Tamaulipas (http://mexgenlink.com/39rz)
- Tlaxcala (http://mexgenlink.com/bd8o)
- Veracruz (http://mexgenlink.com/10km)
- Yucatán (http://mexgenlink.com/xehx)
- Zacatecas (http://mexgenlink.com/yyue)

I hope that you have learned that knowing Mexican history especially local history to be an essential key to unlocking our ancestors past and finding out whom they were.

Always keep in mind, if you don't know where to look for documents on a particular ancestor, but know where he/she used to live. Then it is a clear indication that you need to do your research for that area. Usually records are kept in the city or town that is the head of the municipality. It would be equivalent to your county seat, here in the United States.

What if you don't know where your ancestor was from, but you do have a town and or ranch name. The following section will help you find where it is located in Mexico.

Website to Help You Find Where Your Ancestors Where From In Mexico

While conducting our Mexican Genealogical research you will come across names of haciendas or towns in Mexico that cannot be found on Google maps or anywhere else on the internet. If this is the case then you will really like the following website since it will help you find or at least narrow down the location of where that town or hacienda may be.

Before I go any further I want to thank Jaime Trejo for sharing this amazing tool with us. The website that Jaime shared with us is a Mexican Government website called "Catalogo de Localidades" and it is maintained and hosted by SEDESOL Secretaria de Desarollo Social. You can find the link to visit this website towards the end of this post.

How can you use this tool on your Mexican Genealogy Research?

Very simple, let's say that you know that your ancestors came from Tamaulipas, Mexico and you find a document that indicates that they were born in La Reyna Azteca, Mexico. Good, now you have a name and you try to find it in Google maps only to be taken to a city in

Chile in South America. Obviously that is wrong since you are looking for a town in Tamaulipas, Mexico. Now with the Catalogo de Localidades all you have to do is on the home page of the website is to click Tamaulipas on the map and towards the center of the page you will find in red "Listado de municipios" and to your right hand you will find two excel files available for download. The one titled "Exportar listado de Localidades" is a list of every locality found within that state plus statistical data. Also next to it there is another excel file titled "Exportar listado de Municipios" which is just a list of local municipalities that contains statistical information about them.

After I downloaded the list "Exportar listado de Localidades" I opened it using excel and pressed "CTRL+F" entered La Reyna Azteca and there it was. It showed that it was located in the Municipality of Miguel Aleman, Tamaulipas. If you can't find it use a different spelling and or variation of the name.

Now what do you do with this information?

You do research on the municipality and find the local and historical parishes to find church information on your ancestors. Also do research on the history of the municipality. For example I found out that the Municipality this ranch belongs to is Miguel Aleman. The municipality was created in the 1950's and prior to that it used to be within the municipality of Mier which had been around since the 1750's. Also historically La Reyna Azteca used to belong to the local Mier Parish. Turns out that Civil records for that town are in Mier and not in Miguel Aleman. Also found out that that town started to keep its own civil registry records in 1925 due to the distance from Mier, Tamaulipas.

You can use the same example that I did for every state in Mexico. I also found that areas that have been named are also listed. For example Los Guajillos is an area that covers many miles and many ranches and is not listed in maps but was also listed on the list. I also found many other towns that I have been to in person but do not appear on maps.

Visit Website:

This is the link to the website:

- http://www.microrregiones.gob.mx/catloc/Default.aspx

  (http://mexgenlink.com/k0sz)

Once again thanks Jaime for making me aware of this great resource.

I almost forgot to mention that this resource is great to find localities in modern times. Now, what if you are looking for a ranch, town, or hacienda prior to the 1900's? The resource that I mention in the next section will help you locate them before 1888.

Locating Your Mexican Ancestors Ranch or Town in Mexico Prior to 1888

This resource will help you locate Mexican towns whose name might have had changed after 1888. It will also help you get more details about the towns your ancestors used to reside or live at. The resource I am talking about was written back in 1888 by Antonio García Cubas and it is titled "Diccionario geográfico, histórico y biográfico de los Estados Unidos Mexicanos" (in english "Geographical, Historical and Biographical Dictionary of the United States of Mexico").

The importance of locating towns is imperative when it comes to Mexican Genealogical Research since without a geographic location it will be very difficult to locate documents about your ancestors. In my previous section "Website to Help You Find Where Your Ancestors Where from In Mexico" I describe how you can locate current cities and towns. The problem is that cities and towns do get their names changed. "Geographical, Historical and Biographical Dictionary of the United States of Mexico" will help you locate these towns. Once you locate your ancestor's town you will have a description as to what state and municipality it belongs to, thus giving you an idea where to continue to search for documents.

There are two places online that you can check this resource out by yourself and I list them bellow.

Digital Library of Daniel Cosio Villegas:

What is great about this website is that it contains a list of all the cities and towns for easy browsing.

You can visit it by using this link:

- http://biblio2.colmex.mx/bibdig/dicc_cubas/base3.htm (http://mexgenlink.com/08c2)

Digital Collection of UANL

This is another repository that has this resource online. The only unfortunate thing is that it is very difficult to locate anything but you never know maybe you may prefer it.

You can access it here:

- http://cdigital.dgb.uanl.mx/la/1080011597_C/1080011597_T1/1 080011597_T1.html (http://mexgenlink.com/z5bl)

Up to this point you should have the necessary tools and resources to help you find where your ancestors came from. If you still can't find where they came from don't worry. As you learn in this book about other resources, you will get ideas and or clues as to how to find were they came from in Mexico.

In the following section I will talk about FamilySearch and how it will help you in your research.

FamilySearch, its Search and Online Document Repositories

I will be honest, I am often surprised that a lot of people don't know about <u>FamilySearch.org</u> and the wealth of information that it provides for free. Especially all the Mexican Genealogical Records that it holds. If you are one of these people and have not heard about FamilySearch you are in for a treat.

I have been doing genealogy research for well over fifteen years, but in the last three years I have found more information and ancestors than on the previous eleven years combined and it is all thanks to FamilySearch online digital images.

<u>FamilySearch.org</u> is going online and all digital. They have plans to eventually phase out their microfilm collections by putting all of them online.

What Is FamilySearch.org?

FamilySearch is a genealogy organization operated by The Church of Jesus Christ of Latter-day Saints. It is the largest genealogy organization in the world. FamilySearch maintains a collection of records, resources, and services designed to help people learn more about their family history. FamilySearch gathers, preserves, and shares genealogical records worldwide. It offers free access to its resources and service online at FamilySearch.org, one of the

most heavily used genealogy sites on the Internet. -
Wikipidia.org

The following are all the Document Repositories available at FamilySearch pertaining to Mexican Genealogical Records.

Searchable Databases

The following searchable databases are simply awesome since they are basically an index that will help you find your ancestors. Once you locate them you will be provided with all the necessary information so that you may browse the Church Records to find a copy of the original document.

- <u>Mexico, Baptisms, 1560-1950</u> (http://mexgenlink.com/kqpg) - Church records covering all 32 Mexican States.
- <u>Mexico, Deaths, 1680-1940</u> (http://mexgenlink.com/nkam) - Church records covering all 32 Mexican States.
- <u>Mexico, Marriages, 1570-1950</u> (http://mexgenlink.com/4uyf) - Church records covering all 32 Mexican States.

Browsable Online Catholic Church Record Images

- <u>Catholic Church Records</u> (http://mexgenlink.com/ms17) - This link will take you to a website page where all the Catholic Church Record Repositories at FamilySearch are listed.

To learn how to browse these collections please see the section titled: Find Your Mexican Ancestors Using Mexican Catholic Records

Browsable Online Civil Registration Record Images

- <u>Mexican Civil Registry Records</u> (http://mexgenlink.com/rpr9) - This link will take you to our page where all the Catholic Church Record Repositories at FamilySearch are listed.

To learn how to browse these collections please see the section titled: Find Your Mexican Ancestors Using Civil Registry Documents

How do I Search FamilySearch?

It is very simple to search for an ancestor at FamilySearch.org, to get started type familysearch.org in your browser.

Once you are there, towards the middle of the home page you will see an icon, a laptop with magnifying glass, labeled Search. Just click it, this will send you straight to their search page.

What I do is enter the last name of the ancestor that I am looking for and I either enter the spouses name or the parent's names. This type of combination will return more relevant searches.

If you don't happen to know the names of the parents or spouse enter a location or year range when your ancestor lived. Be creative enter all types of combinations with all the information that you may have.

In the following sections I will be talking about both Civil and Church records that are available at FamilySearch. Before we do that in the next section I will provide you with tools and resources that will help you transcribe and help you also read these hand written documents.

Resources to Help You Decipher Mexican Church and Civil Records

Once you find your first documents on FamilySearch and overcome the joy of finding them. It can be discouraging that you may not be able to decipher them. I mean decipher since some are very hard to read, especially when you do not know what the document contains. I won't lie to you some are super easy to read but there are some that it does take considerable skill and knowledge. It took me several months of practice to really start transcribing documents with ease.

Even at that I cannot transcribe all Spanish documents, the ones I have no problems with are Mexican Church, and Civil documents. Don't tell me to transcribe any other Spanish speaking country because I can't.

Here are the sources that I used to learn to transcribe Mexican Spanish Church and Civil Registry Documents. The tutorials are provided free of charge by BYU (Brigham Young University) Center for Family History and Genealogy. The following tutorial will help you get familiarized with Spanish parish records. It also contains an index of given names, surnames, abbreviations, Glossary of Spanish terms, occupations, and racial designations

Check the tutorial here, you can choose between Spanish and English

English Tutorial (http://mexgenlink.com/oqxt)

Spanish Tutorial (http://mexgenlink.com/ninc)

Other Excellent Guides

Spanish Genealogical Word List
(http://mexgenlink.com/h1eh) - This list contains Spanish words
with their English translations. The words included here are those
that you are likely to find in genealogical sources.

Transcription Rules &
Techniques (http://mexgenlink.com/ahyo) – This is a great article on
Abstracting & Transcribing Genealogical Documents, By Kimberly
Powell.

Software to Help You Out

Use Transcript2.3 (http://mexgenlink.com/korr) it is free
or you can use Genscriber (http://mexgenlink.com/ak5h) depending
on your needs, it is also free for personal noncommercial use.
Genscriber is also available for the Mac. I personally use Transcript
2.3.

I know that you will find all these resources useful and
helpful towards reading and transcribing documents. At first, as I
mentioned before, it will be hard and sometimes frustrating but don't
get discouraged. It takes practice to learn how to transcribe them.
Also always use other records on the same page to help you out. In
some instances you will find patterns that will help you out.

In the following section you will learn about Mexican Civil
Registry records and the wealth of genealogical information that
they contain.

Find Your Mexican Ancestors Using Civil Registry Documents

With this section I will show you how to find your ancestors using Civil Registry Documents with techniques and examples that have worked for me in my own quest of finding my ancestors.

Brief Civil Registry History

Just for those of you whom are not familiar with El Registro Civil or the Civil Registry let me give you some background information. During Spanish rule and sometime after its independence Mexico's vital records were kept by the Catholic Church from about the 1500's up until 1860's. Of course some states started to keep records even before 1860. What happened was that in 1860 or 1859, Benito Juarez the president of Mexico at the time declared that all vital records Birth, Marriage, and Death records had to be kept by the state. Church records would no longer be valid for government transactions. Thus the Registro Civil was created.

Ok, good, we are done with my sketchy history let's move along to the good stuff.

Where to Find Mexican Civil Registry Records Online

The first thing and most important thing you need to know is that FamilySearch has made the civil registry records accessible online for most of the Mexican States and you can access them from here Civil Registry (http://mexgenlink.com/rpr9), but don't go there just yet. Most of these records span from 1859 to mostly 1930's due to privacy laws, but I have found some records up until 2005. Another thing you need to be aware of is that most of these records are also copies of the originals that the Civil Registry official had to send to the state capital at the end of each year. Due to this reason most of these documents don't contain the original signatures of our ancestors since the originals are still on the shelves of the local Civil Registration offices at the municipality level.

Unfortunately, this gold mine of records has not been indexed (some states have been indexed) and the search for your ancestors has to be done manually. I say gold mine since these records contain the following:

- **Birth:** Name of child, and time of birth. Names of parents, age, occupation and where they were from. Names of grandparents and where they were from.
- **Marriage Licenses:** Names of couple, their age. Names of parents and sometimes their age. Location of marriage and names of witnesses.
- **Marriage:** Names of couple, date of marriage announcement, their age. Names of parents and sometimes their age. Location of marriage and names of witnesses.
- **Death:** Location of death, burial, occupation, name of spouse, name of parents, and location of burial.

How to Browse or Download Mexican Civil Registry Images

When I first started to research these records I discovered that most of the years had indexes at the front or end of each year. Soon I discovered that if I divided the pages by years of any particular collection I could estimate the number of pages that the indexes were located on or about every # of pages then with the dates on the documents I would either go forward or backward to locate the index. For example, if the collection contained 500 pages and covered 10 years I would divide 500 by 10 thus getting 50. This is a simple way and somewhat faster than searching page by page.

Once you find their name next to it there will be a number labeled *Acta* this is the Record entry number. Just look for that number within those years pages and you will find his Birth record. You can use this same method to look for a death, or marriage record.

If the town you are looking for is not listed on the Civil Registry records do a Google search and locate the biggest town around it. More than likely that's were your ancestors had to register, but if you want to be more accurate do a locality research on the history of the town and *Municipio (*county) boundaries.

How I Found My Maternal 2nd Great Grandparents

I had been searching for my Maternal 2nd Great grandparents for years and had no luck in finding out their names. It wasn't until I located them thanks to the Civil Registration records available at FamilySearch that I did learn their names.

So the family had neither documents nor clues as to whom they were or their names. I only had the names for my great grandparents but not birth dates for them. I first searched for my great grandparents small Mexican town of Los Trevino's but it would not even come up on Google, fortunately I had been to that town a few years ago and I knew its location and was able to find it Google maps. I then looked at the nearest towns and there was only Ciudad Miguel Aleman, and Ciudad Mier. After some research I learned that Ciudad Miguel Aleman was founded in 1950 so there was no way they had what I was looking for even though Los Trevinos belonged to its jurisdiction. After some more research I found out that Ciudad Mier was founded in 1753 and Los Trevinos was in land that used to belong to Ciudad Mier's jurisdiction before 1950. I quickly found the Civil Registration Records for Ciudad Mier in the State of Tamaulipas.

I then figured that since my grandmother was born in 1925 I should at least look 10 years prior for the marriage of my Great grandparents. So I found the index of 1915 and did not find them. Then on the one for 1916 I found them with Acta 4 next to them. I quickly browsed my way to number four and there is was. It was page and half document about their marriage. It had their ages, occupation, and best of all the names of four new ancestors. As you can see these records can be the key to finding your ancestors.

These are the following states that are available for browsing:

I have listed here all the Civil Registry records available at FamilySearch for your convenience.

- Baja California and Baja California Sur, Civil Registration, 1860-2004 (http://mexgenlink.com/hp3m) Browse Only.
- Campeche, Civil Registration, 1860-1926 (http://mexgenlink.com/u38j) Browse Only
- Chiapas, Civil Registration, 1861-1990 (http://mexgenlink.com/s6xc) Browse Only
- Chihuahua, Civil Registration, 1861-1997 (http://mexgenlink.com/3flf) Searchable
- Coahuila, Civil Registration, 1861-1998 (http://mexgenlink.com/e29o) Searchable
- Colima, Civil Registration, 1860-1997 (http://mexgenlink.com/jrp9) Browse Only
- Distrito Federal, Civil Registration, 1832-2005 (http://mexgenlink.com/2s56) Browse Only
- Durango, Civil Registration, 1861-1995 (http://mexgenlink.com/twh0) Browse Only
- Guanajuato, Civil Registration, 1862-1930 (http://mexgenlink.com/pyrs) Browse Only
- Guerrero, Civil Registration, 1833-1996 (http://mexgenlink.com/69b1) Searchable
- Hidalgo, Civil Registration, 1861-1967 (http://mexgenlink.com/a8o1) Browse Only
- Jalisco, Civil Registration, 1857-2000 (http://mexgenlink.com/e2gy) Browse Only
- Michoacán, Civil Registration, 1859-1940 (http://mexgenlink.com/otz2) Browse Only
- Morelos, Civil Registration, 1861-1920 (http://mexgenlink.com/20y5) Browse Only

- México Estado, Civil Registration, 1861-1941 (http://mexgenlink.com/3xc3) Browse Only
- Mexico, Civil Registration, 1860-1950 (http://mexgenlink.com/8d16) - Tlaxcala and Aguascalientes, Searchable
- Nayarit, Civil Registration, 1868-2001 (http://mexgenlink.com/fplo) Browse Only
- Nuevo León, Civil Registration, 1859-1962 (http://mexgenlink.com/0rrz) Browse Only
- Oaxaca, Civil Registration, 1861-2002 (http://mexgenlink.com/j580) Browse Only
- Puebla, Civil Registration, 1861-1930 (http://mexgenlink.com/u808) Browse Only
- Querétaro, Civil Registration, 1864-2005 (http://mexgenlink.com/hjao) Browse Only
- Quintana Roo, Civil Registration, 1866-1902 (http://mexgenlink.com/4duh) Browse Only
- San Luis Potosí, Civil Registration, 1859-2000 (http://mexgenlink.com/upwy) Searchable
- San Luis Potosí, Miscellaneous Records, 1570-1842 (http://mexgenlink.com/akaw) Searchable
- Sonora, Civil Registration, 1861-1995 (http://mexgenlink.com/h1lr) Browse Only
- Tabasco, Catholic Church Records, 1803-1970 (http://mexgenlink.com/0m9i) Browse Only
- Tamaulipas, Civil Registration, 1800-2002 (http://mexgenlink.com/mduw) Browse Only
- Veracruz, Civil Registration, 1821-1949 (http://mexgenlink.com/h6g2) Browse Only
- Yucatán, Civil Registration. 1860-1926 (http://mexgenlink.com/y3q4) Browse Only
- Zacatecas, Civil Registration, 1860-2000 (http://mexgenlink.com/9fox) Browse Only

Now that you are aware of the Civil Registry records available at FamilySearch in the next section you will learn about Catholic Church records that are available also at FamilySearch.

Find Your Mexican Ancestors Using Mexican Catholic Church Records

Mexican Church Records the Low Hanging Fruit

Mexican Catholic Church records are what I like to think the low hanging fruit in Mexican Genealogy research since they are, in my opinion, the easiest records to find. In this post I will show you where to search and browse Catholic Church Marriage, Baptism, and Death records in order to find your ancestors and ancestry. These records are also very valuable since they date from as early as 1560 up until the 1950's. These records preceded the Mexican Civil Registry records.

Thanks to FamilySearch.org most of these records have already been indexed and are available online from anywhere in the world. Unfortunately some parishes have not been indexed but I will give you some ideas where to find indexes for those areas. For your convenience you can access all these records available at FamilySearch from this page at mexicangenealogy.info Church Records Page (http://mexgenlink.com/ms17) or from the end of this section.

Abbreviations

Before we get more in-depth let me just warn you about name variations. Since these records go back hundreds of years back up until the 1500's and in some locations, the way names used to be written has changed. The older the documents you will find that Jose was written as Joseph and Javier as Xavier. Also be aware of abbreviations such as Jph for Joseph, Ma. for Maria, and Fraco/Franca, for Francisco/Francisca. You might also want to download and see the following PDF, Spanish Name Abbreviations (http://mexgenlink.com/jnic), for more examples. When reading the old documents also keep in mind that a lot of common words or even places were abbreviated.

Searching Mexican Church Records at FamilySearch

The primary place to search for your ancestors is FamilySearch.org since they have indexed most Church collections, but if you don't find them there do not be discouraged since I will also tell you about other alternatives. For your convenience you can find the links to search for Marriage, Baptism, and Death record from mexicangenealogy.info Church Records Page (http://mexgenlink.com/ms17). They are also available at the end of this section.

Searching Marriage Records

To search I always enter the grooms name and also wife's name, if their names are not that common you will only get a few results but if they are very common you will get several. When you get several or too many, look at the dates and location of the records to find you ancestors. Once you find the indexed record you will only see the basic information indexed and most of the time the parents will be listed. If they are not listed don't worry it does not mean that their names are not on the original document, many times they are. You can search for Marriages here Mexico, Marriages, 1570-1950 (http://mexgenlink.com/4uyf).

Searching Baptism Records

Once you find the names of your ancestor from their marriage record the next step is to find his/her baptism record. To do this, just enter the names of the parents and hopefully your ancestors baptism will be along with the ones of his siblings. Once again if the names are common which is not that common, narrow it down with place and dates. You can search for Baptisms here Mexico, Baptisms, 1560-1950 (http://mexgenlink.com/kqpg).

Searching Death Records

Death Records are a bit hard to locate since sometimes the only name on the record is of the deceased. That is the reason that it is harder to narrow it down. There may be many results with the same name but again narrow it down to location and date. Also try entering the husband/wife name or parents and you will sometimes find it that way. You can search for Death records here Mexico Deaths, 1680-1940 (http://mexgenlink.com/nkam).

You Have a Date Then What

Unfortunately most indexed records do not have a link to the copy of the original image. So now we will browse FamilySearch Mexican Collections (http://mexgenlink.com/0n7e) to locate the document and I will demonstrate this with an example.

I had been searching for my third great grandparents for years but could never locate them on the Municipality of Mier Tamaulipas where my Marroquin family was from in Mexico. Then I tried searching for them in FamilySearch and got a result Jo. Angl. Marroquin and Franca. Perez for Allende, Nuevo Leon. At the time I had no idea about common abbreviations and did not know it was them so I ignored it. Then about a year after I learned about abbreviations these names came back to me and I searched for them again. This time the same record came back plus my second great grandfather's baptism record came back listed with several of his siblings as well. At this point I knew I had the right couple. I also learned a very important lesson, always come back to see if more records have been added, since I am assuming that the first time the baptism records for that locality had not been indexed yet.

I then got the date for the marriage record, and went browsing. To browse these I first went to familysearch.org / Search /

Mexico / Mexico, Nuevo León, Catholic Church Records, 1667-1981 / Browse through 447,381 images / Allende / San Pedro Apostol and finally Matrimonios 1857-1905 (http://mexgenlink.com/e0il). Once there it took me a few minute to locate the record for 1865 since they are in order by date it was not that difficult.

After I read it I found out that the names were also abbreviated in the original document and that the parents for both of my ancestors were listed there but for whatever reason they were not indexed. This is why it is very important to always get a copy of the original document.

Through further research of church marriage, baptisms and death records I found out that my Marroquin were from the Allende, Santiago, and Monterrey area and have traced them back till the 1600's just with church records.

FamilySearch Has Not Indexed Everything

FamilySearch has not indexed everything, this is very important to remember, for examples in my area of research Ciudad Camargo, Tamaulipas and Cerralvo, Nuevo Leon have not been indexed. The great thing is that FamilySearch does have their images online for browsing.

When I can't find my ancestors in FamilySearch I always search for them in Google, you will be surprised. Many times someone else has already done research on them. For example Raul Longoria (http://raullongoria.net) has thousands of people listed for these two areas and I use his research to locate the original images. You might also want to search for books that may already have those records indexed. Examples of these types of books are the ones offered by the (Spanish American Genealogical Association). SAGA (http://www.sagacorpuschristi.com). You might also want to check out your local University Library for genealogical books pertaining to the city or town where your ancestors lived. In my case I have found over 100 books where at least one of my ancestors is named and in some instances they are the focus of the whole book. These books have provided me with dates to locate copies of original images. An example of these books is <u>Los Marroquin de el Valle de Santiago del Guaxuco</u> (http://mexgenlink.com/pxxz), I found it in my local University. I will discuss more about books in a later section.

You now have the necessary knowledge and an example on how to locate your ancestors using Catholic Church records. The most important thing to remember is that these records are available at <u>FamilySearch.org</u> or you can access them form here.

Browsable image Collections by State:

These are all the Mexico Church collections that are available at FamilySearch for church records.

- <u>Aguascalientes, Catholic Church Records, 1620-1962</u> (http://mexgenlink.com/rciy)
- <u>Baja California and Baja California Sur, Catholic Church Records, 1750-1984</u> (http://mexgenlink.com/f1ik)
- <u>Campeche, Catholic Church Records, 1638-1944</u> (http://mexgenlink.com/1wx2)
- <u>Chiapas, Catholic Church Records, 1558-1978</u> (http://mexgenlink.com/3zou)
- <u>Chihuahua, Catholic Church Records, 1632-1958</u> (http://mexgenlink.com/2d10)
- <u>Coahuila, Catholic Church Records, 1627-1978</u> (http://mexgenlink.com/dgpt)
- <u>Colima, Catholic Church Records, 1707-1969</u> (http://mexgenlink.com/2qxk)
- <u>Distrito Federal, Catholic Church Records, 1886-1933</u> (http://mexgenlink.com/zo55)
- <u>Durango, Catholic Church Records, 1604-1985</u> (http://mexgenlink.com/2cig) Searchable
- <u>Guanajuato, Catholic Church Records, 1576-1984</u> (http://mexgenlink.com/cw2h)
- <u>Guerrero, Catholic Church Records, 1576-1979</u> (http://mexgenlink.com/qhss)

- Hidalgo, Catholic Church Records, 1546-1971 (http://mexgenlink.com/bhvr) Searchable
- Jalisco, Catholic Church Records, 1590-1995 (http://mexgenlink.com/yp3q)
- Michoacán, Catholic Church Records, 1649-1909 (http://mexgenlink.com/flvu)
- Morelos, Catholic Church Records, 1598-1969 (http://mexgenlink.com/wv5o)
- Nayarit, Catholic Church Records, 1596-1967 (http://mexgenlink.com/9vr8)
- Nuevo León, Catholic Church Records, 1667-1981 (http://mexgenlink.com/m6mk)
- Oaxaca, Catholic Church Records, 1559-1988 (http://mexgenlink.com/ckam)
- Puebla, Catholic Church Records, 1545-1970 (http://mexgenlink.com/pp40) Searchable
- Querétaro, Catholic Church Records, 1590-1970 (http://mexgenlink.com/gq32) Searchable
- San Luis Potosí, Catholic Church Records, 1586-1970 (http://mexgenlink.com/y2v6)
- Sinaloa, Catholic Church Records, 1671-1968 (http://mexgenlink.com/vm91)
- Sonora, Catholic Church Records, 1657-1994 (http://mexgenlink.com/lt9d) Searchable
- State of Mexico, Catholic Church Records (http://mexgenlink.com/rtgr)
- Tabasco, Catholic Church Records, 1803-1970 (http://mexgenlink.com/ofcb)
- Tamaulipas, Catholic Church Records, 1703-1964 (http://mexgenlink.com/i2o9)
- Tlaxcala, Catholic Church Records, 1576-1994 (http://mexgenlink.com/nz5o)
- Veracruz, Catholic Church Records, 1590-1970 (http://mexgenlink.com/f42g)
- Yucatán, Catholic Church Records, 1543-1977 (http://mexgenlink.com/dip7)
- Zacatecas, Catholic Church Records, 1605-1980 (http://mexgenlink.com/yvnb) Searchable

You will eventually learn that Church records are indispensable for your research. In the next section I will talk to you about something that goes hand in hand with marriage records and that is marriage dispensations.

How to Locate Your Mexican Ancestor's Marriage Dispensation

What is a marriage dispensation? In short, couples that wished to get married and had any type of relationship by blood between them had to request a marriage dispensation from the church. This was done for marriages between cousins, uncles and nieces, and distant cousins. There are many other types of relationships but you get the idea.

I was doing some research on my wife's family and came across the marriage record for her sixth great grandparents dated 7-28-1732 and the record indicated that they had a dispensation in the 3rd degree. They married in Monterrey, Nuevo Leon, Mexico. This aroused my interest as to how they were related and especially since I was missing their grandparent's names.

The first thing I did was open up the book "Index to the Marriage Investigations of the Diocese of Guadalajara 1653 - 1750" (http://mexgenlink.com/1mnt) and looked for their names in the index of names located on the back of the book. I knew that they had to be there and sure enough entree 42-6 was theirs. It indicated that the dispensation took place in Monterrey back in May 2, 1732 and best of all it showed exactly how they were related. That's it, I could have stopped here but no, I decided that I wanted to get a copy of the original document.

At the top of the page in the book it indicated that it came from microfilm #0168116 and the entry indicated that the dispensation was number 48. I also happened to know that Monterrey was under the diocese of Gudalajara up until 1779. With this information I quickly headed to FamilySearch's online records for Gudalajara (http://mexgenlink.com/c61h) and located the Marriages for 1731 - 1732, I made sure I had the correct film number and once I verified this I started to search for the image.

Unfortunately they were not in order and after half an hour on page 217 I found it, five images containing 10 pages of handwritten writing. It contained a treasure trove of information that detailed exactly how they were related to each other.

As I have showed it is not that hard to locate a marriage dispensation.

Before I forget if you do not have access to the book "Index to the Marriage Investigations of the Diocese of Guadalajara 1653 - 1750" (http://mexgenlink.com/1mnt) I recommend you try and find your ancestors corresponding film number and dispensation number at Guadalajara Dispensas (http://www.guadalajaradispensas.com). This is a great website where they are slowly indexing all the microfilms available at family search. The purpose of the project is to help everyone more easily locate marriage dispensations. Just remember that they are still indexing films, in-case you don't find them there.

Another thing to keep in mind is that you have to do some research about the church you are trying to find the dispensations for. Either search on Google or read a book about that particular church. A good example of this was that I could not locate one for one of my ancestors in the *dispensas* of Guadalajara. It turned out that for my particular town they were next to the marriage records labeled as *Informacion Matrimonial* on FamilySearch and for whatever reason they were not sent to Guadalajara. Finally, keep in mind also that after 1779 other archdioceses were created. Each archdiocese would have had kept their own records.

Now that you have a basic knowledge of marriage dispensations and know where to look for them I will, in the next section, talk about Civil Registry databases. These will help you find more recent relatives.

Using Mexican Civil Registry Databases to Find Your Mexican Ancestors

Another great resource that I have used to do my own family genealogy research time and time again are the Civil Registration Databases that many Mexican States have set up in an effort to modernize their records and are free to the general public. I will be talking mainly about the Civil Registry website for Tamaulipas since this is the main one that I use but the searching methods are similar to all other websites. At the end of this section I will also provide you with a list to all the state databases that I have found to date.

The main thing to keep in mind is that these databases generally only cover from 1930 to the present and they are for birth, marriage, and death records. Sometimes you will also find divorce and adoption databases. You might also find earlier births but only if the birth was recorded after the 1930's as one of the following examples shows. You will also find them if the marriage occurred years after the couple eloped they may also be found if they married after the 1930's. These databases are also great to find information about your uncles and cousins that is if they were born in Mexico.

Description of databases:

The Tamaulipas database has births, marriages, and deaths. Once you are in the page it will let you select between Nacimientos (births) and Matrimonios, (marriages). For example if you chose births it will provide you with a drop down list to choose a municipality (municipio). Once you select it you just need to enter the persons date of birth and you will be provided with an unofficial record. For example, the Tamaulipas database will provide you with vital information as well as the parent's names and where they were from. I mainly use this database to get concrete evidence and citations for my own family database. Since I am sure that if I ask family members for their birth certificate they would probably think I am crazy.

Tip: If your ancestor died after 1930 and have a date of birth you might want to look for them since if they were registered after 1930 you will find their information here. That's how I found the parents of one of my ancestors. He was born in 1909 but was registered in 1956.

Other Mexican Civil Registry Databases

All the other databases use similar search criteria, but whatever you do just play with the search function and try it with different individuals. If you don't find one don't be discouraged just keep in mind that the data was entered by humans and it does contain errors such as misspelled names and thus that might be the reason that you don't find what you are looking for.

Here are the databases that I have found up to this date. You can always find an updated list of the following at Civil Registry (http://mexgenlink.com/rpr9).

Searchable State Civil Registry Databases:

- Coahuila Civil Registry Births (http://mexgenlink.com/cq9w)
- Coahuila Civil Registry Deaths (http://mexgenlink.com/do4j)
- Coahuila Civil Registry Divorces (http://mexgenlink.com/pa3q)
- Coahuila Civil Registry Marriages (http://mexgenlink.com/wm4p)
- Colima Civil Registry Births (http://mexgenlink.com/pa4i)

- Colima Civil Registry Deaths (http://mexgenlink.com/vnuo)
- Colima Civil Registry Divorces (http://mexgenlink.com/ilbw)
- Colima Civil Registry Marriages (http://mexgenlink.com/140e)
- Guerrero Civil Registry Births (http://mexgenlink.com/lzi8)
- Guerrero Civil Registry Marriages (http://mexgenlink.com/g048)
- Guerrero Civil Registry Deaths (http://mexgenlink.com/tezi)
- Tamaulipas Civil Registry Births (http://mexgenlink.com/4iao)
- Tamaulipas Civil Registry Marriages (http://mexgenlink.com/n532)

Unfortunately the above states are the only ones that I have found and they do change from time to time. Nuevo Leon used to have one but in one year it has been removed and is no longer online.

In the following section I will talk to you about border crossing records. They are an excellent resource to help you find ancestors, the place where your ancestor was from in Mexico, and if you are lucky you might even find a photo of them.

Using the Mexican Border Crossing Records in Your Mexican Ancestry Research

In some cases not all, but maybe in your case, searching the Mexican Border Crossing Records could be the key to finding your ancestors. I have found that if your family immigrated to the United States between 1895 and 1957 chances are that you will find your ancestors using these records.

These records are great since once you find a record it will contain various details about your ancestors, specially the date and place of birth. These records will also provide us with clues as to where else to search for him or her. Also these records may contain your ancestors fingerprint, in some cases even a photo, names of parents, and also names of people that were traveling with them.

An example of how I used these Records

Some time back I could not locate the correct wife for one of my grandmother's brothers. The problem was that the small town that they were from had several women living by the same name during the same time period.

When the border crossing records became available online I searched for my grandmothers brother, just to record if he had ever crossed to the United States and he did. I found a border crossing for him where he listed his wife's name as the person accompanying him.

I have a habit of always looking at the record before and after the one that I find. When I did this, in this case, the record after his was the one for his wife. The record provided me with allot of information it even listed her parents.

Of course this all would have had been avoided if my father had known whom the parents of his uncles wife were but he did not or if we would have had a way of contacting one of her living sons. This only shows the importance of first trying to get the information with family.

I have also used these records to determine where some of my ancestors were from.

Mexican Border Crossing Records Online

You can use the following resources to learn more about these records and also search for your ancestors.

- <u>National Archives</u> (http://mexgenlink.com/p9kv) - Here you will find a brief introduction about the Mexican Border Crossings, how and why immigration records were collected, special conditions on the Mexican Border, immigration statistics and definitions, who's in the records, the types of forms used, available microfilm publications and where to find NARA microfilm.

- <u>United States, Border Crossings from Mexico to United States, 1903-1957</u> (http://mexgenlink.com/wy9d) - This is a searchable collection that contains 3,610,754 records of immigration records from various ports along the United States Mexico Border. They are courtesy of Ancestry.com

- Border Crossings: From Mexico to U.S., 1895-1957 (http://mexgenlink.com/cjks) – This resource is the best of all three since you can search and also browse the images. You can actually see your ancestor's signature and sometimes even their thumb print. The only thing is that in order to use this resource you will need a membership which costs about $19.95 per month; they do offer a 14 day free trial.

Learn More about Border Crossings 1895 to 1957

- Crossing the Frontera (http://mexgenlink.com/ym23) – If your ancestor crossed the U.S. border from Mexico between 1895 and 1957, you may want to try searching for them in Border Crossing records available at FamilySearch. This class will give you a little background information about the records and their content. It will also show you how they can be used to identify your ancestor's home town in Mexico. The class includes a case study and important search tips and techniques.

I know that these records will be as useful to you as they have been for me.

Another great resource that will be very useful to finding your ancestors is the 1930 Mexican Census. In the next section you will learn more about it.

Using the 1930 Mexican Census to Find Your Mexican Ancestors

The Mexico Census of 1930 is the 5th Mexican national census and it is a great resource to help you find your ancestors. I personally have been lucky in finding other peoples ancestors using this census.

Before you go searching let me just warn you that this census only contains 90% of the population. Unfortunately my family, through both sides, is not in it. I searched, but the Municipality they resided at is nowhere to be found. I am not sure if it was an indexing problem, if those pages got lost, or they were simply not enumerated. Well I hope your case is not my case and you do find your ancestors.

As I mentioned before I have been lucky to have found other peoples ancestors in this census. An example was when I was looking for my brother in laws ancestors. The census provided me with the location they were from and also the whole family of his grandparents and great grandparents. Thanks to the information obtained from this census I was able to trace his family to the early 1800's.

The following are two resources where you can search the 1930 Mexico Census for free.

To Search the 1930 Mexico Census

- Ancestry (http://mexgenlink.com/1tl4) - 1930 Mexico National Census El Quinto Censo General de Población y Vivienda 1930, México

- FamilySearch (http://mexgenlink.com/exg0) - Mexico Census, 1930

For More Information about the 1930 Mexico Census

- FamilySearch Wiki (http://mexgenlink.com/14uc)

I hope that you give this resource a try since it is very useful to help you locate ancestors and also provide you with location that they were from in Mexico that is if you don't know that yet.

If you did not find your ancestors don't worry they may appear in newspapers and in the next section I will show you were to look for them.

Finding Your Mexican Ancestors in Newspapers

Sometimes your ancestors made it into the pages of newspapers and these stories are full of details and information. They are a window to our ancestor's lives. Some articles may even contain a photo of them. The question of where to look for Mexican Ancestors in newspapers comes up very often and that is why I have included this section.

I'll be clear, you might search and not find anything as was the case with my own family but who knows it might be different with your family and you might actually find them. The only wrong thing you could do is not even try to search for them. I realized how important newspaper stories could be when I was doing research for a client and I hit a gold mine of information regarding their ancestors. The newspaper was from the El Paso area and their family moving to the city was a big deal that made it into the papers. Then you see that they quickly became part of the social sphere for El Paso and thus appeared on the newspaper often.

Many clues that I found there helped take the research to a specific location in Mexico. This information provided me with what I needed to research this particular family's birth and marriage records.

I will list the Newspaper resources that I know of, but let me advise you I am sure there are many more out there.

Free Newspaper Resources

Chronicling America

- Chronicling America is a Website providing access to information about historic newspapers and select digitized newspaper pages, and is a long-term effort to develop an Internet-based, searchable database of U.S. newspapers with descriptive information and select digitization of historic pages.

Visit Website: http://chroniclingamerica.loc.gov/

Google Newspapers Archives

- Contains thousands of Newspapers worldwide and have many of the newspapers for Border States of the United States.

Visit Website: http://news.google.com/newspapers

The Portal to Texas History

This is one of my favorite websites due to the amount of research and historical information that I have been able to find. I have even found several articles about my wife's family.

Visit Website: http://texashistory.unt.edu/

Elephind

- Elephind is a search engine like Google, but it is designed for searching historic digitized newspaper collections. According to its website it currently searches more than 140 million newspaper items from the United States, Australia, New Zealand, and elsewhere.

Visit Website: http://www.elephind.com/

Other Available independent Newspapers

- El Informador (http://hemeroteca.informador.com.mx) (1917-)
- El Siglo de Torreón (http://mexgenlink.com/pl47) (1922–2000) -
- El Universal (http://mexgenlink.com/d7f4) (1999–)

Paid Newspaper Resources

Genealogy Bank

- I have personally used Genealogy Bank and I have found great information. They have a seven day free trial.

Visit Website: http://www.genealogybank.com/gbnk/newspapers/

News Papers

- This is another paid service that might be able to help you out. Unfortunately I have not tested it out and have yet to do it, but I am listing it here since I have heard great things about it.

Visit Website: http://www.newspapers.com/

I hope that the above list of places to search for your Mexican ancestors helps you get started in this area of genealogical research. I just wished that more Mexican Newspapers would be digitized but who knows what the future holds. Another thing that I do not want to leave out and highly recommend is to search your local library for any newspapers from Mexico. You never know what you may find. An example of what I am talking about is to check out Yale's collection "Historical Newspapers from 19th century Mexico" (http://mexgenlink.com/qqby).

What the Future Holds

I am guessing that eventually Mexican state archives will digitize newspapers. I know this since that is the case for Tamaulipas. They have over one million digitized pages but as their archivist told me they lack the infrastructure to put them online. Also the Archives of Saltillo are doing the same.

Sometimes our ancestors made it to the newspapers, and I hope that the resources that I have mentioned here help you to find them. Another great resource is obituaries and since we are talking about newspapers in the next section I will talk about using obituaries to find your ancestors.

Find Your Mexican Ancestors Using Obituaries

There are many road blocks when researching your genealogy especially for us of Mexican ancestry residing in the United States; it can be a little more challenging. Sometimes our family refuses to talk about our ancestors or everyone has already passed away. Many of us are second or third generation Americans and have never visited our ancestor's place of origin and do not know where they were from in Mexico. All we know is that they were from Mexico.

That is the reason that I get the following question allot. How can I trace my family to Mexico when I have no clue from what part of Mexico they were from? There are many solutions to try and figure this out and you have already learned about several ways. Now the one I am going to tell you about is using obituaries to find additional clues to help you find your ancestry. I will also show you where to look for obituaries and even how you can get notices to your email inbox.

Obituaries usually contain a great deal of information. I have come across some that are short biographies and others are practically full family trees. Before I go any further let me just warn you that you will also find the type of obituaries that I don't like and those are the ones that are basically just a name, death date, and funeral home information.

Let's just hope that you do find one of the first two mentioned. Obituaries usually will contain a picture, birthday, death date, parent's information, sometimes grandparents, and sibling information. Many will also have a place where major life events occurred, especially birth and death. They also contain cemetery information and funeral home information.

Some time back one of my blog readers sent me and inquiry on how to obtain her mother's great-grandparents information and advised me that her parents as well as her grandparents were all deceased and that all her aunts/uncles and great aunts/uncles where also deceased. I asked where did your parents die and she informed me that they died in the U.S. and that she was first Generation born in the U.S. She also advised that her grandparents died in Mexico. I asked did any siblings of your grandmother ever come to the U.S. and she said yes. I asked have you searched for their obituary and she said no. I provided her with the information of where she could look at and a couple of days later she replied that she found a grandaunt that had just died in 2010 at the fruitful old age of 98. She was much exited since the obituary had the names of her great grandparents and the town where her grandaunt was born in Mexico. She said that it provided her with the clues that she needed to find more generations.

I am very well aware that this might not be the case for you but if you have not dived into searching for obituaries I highly recommend that you do. You may be asking yourself well this is great and all but where should I go looking next.

My Favorite Place to Find Obituaries and The one I Recommend

- Legacy.com – Legacy is by far the best free source out there for obituaries. Sometimes you might have to pay a small fee to view an obituary.

At Legacy's website there is a search box where you enter your ancestors name and last name or the information of whom ever you are searching for. You can also enter a keyword, for example name of a town or other possible last name, perfect for searching for females. Make sure to play with the drop down menu if you leave it as it is you will only be searching for the past 3 days. I always like to use "All Records". Make sure and play with it and try as many different combinations as you can. Try searching for a town using keywords only to see all deaths for that particular town.

Legacy also lets you create obituary alerts. On the home page of legacy's website it says "ObitMessenger" when you visit legacy just click there and signup. It is a free service and the way that I use it is to monitor certain towns from Mexico. I enter the towns as keywords so whenever that town is mentioned on an obituary I get an alert to my email and I can visit it. I have found many distant cousins of my father and grandfather that have died in the U.S. You can even enter names or last names as keywords.

Keep in mind that Legacy.com is for more recent obituaries and you can find some as old as 1939.

Other places to find Obituaries

- <u>Chronicling America Historic American Newspapers</u> (http://chroniclingamerica.loc.gov) – Library of congress project where you can find newspapers as old as 1836.

- <u>Archives.com</u> – Has over 2.6 billion record online and has many obituaries. This one is not free and you do have to pay about $8.00 per month after their free 7 day trial.

- <u>The Portal to Texas History</u> (http://texashistory.unt.edu) – Contains over 11,000 obituaries for Texas.

As you can see finding an obituary can help you bring down some of your brick-walls in your Mexico Genealogy research. After reading this section you now have a basic foundation where to start searching for obituaries, where to sign up for alerts, and three other resources that may help you locate obituaries.

On a final note don't limit yourself to the resources that I mention in here. They are a great place to start but if you have no luck try searching for other newspaper or obituary archives since I know that there are many other ones out there. Try searching for your ancestor on Google and type the word "obituary" next to it. I have been able to find some this way.

Now that we have talked about obituaries and you have the resources to set up notices and or search for your ancestors it is time to talk about death certificates.

Using Death Certificates to Find Your Mexican Ancestors

Another great resource to finding our ancestors for those of us residing in the U.S. is Death Certificates. Yes Death Certificates can provide us with a great wealth of information especially with the names of the parents of our deceased ancestor; sometimes you will even find a place of birth in Mexico or the place of birth of the parents.

A Death Certificate may be the difference between finding your ancestors or not. There are several places where one may obtain Death Certificates. One option is the old fashioned way of going to your local county court house with the county clerk and the other is my favorite familysearch.org since it is online and free.

I will not be talking about the first option since I have never used it but I know that it is available. I just mentioned it since in some cases it may be your only option since many records are still not online on FamilySearch. Luckily for me all of my wife's ancestors were from Texas and thus I have been lucky enough with FamilySearch.

For the longest time my wife's great grandfather was one of my brick walls. I could not locate who his parents were. Since my father in law never got to know their names neither. I searched for the longest time but could not locate his death record. I searched and searched since I always had the hopes that his death certificate would contain the clues that I needed. I knew that he had died in Starr County and that his mother's last name was Lozano. One day, for whatever reason, I searched for him with his mother's last name of Lozano. Instead of Francisco Perez I typed Francisco Lozano and there it was listed as Francisco Perez Lozano. I then typed Francisco Perez Lozano and nothing came up. I thought it was weird and it only shows that we have to be creative when searching for our ancestors.

The death certificate provided me with immense clues, not to mention the names of his parents Encarnacion Perez and Dorotea Lozano. Unfortunately it did not mention his birth place only that he was born in Mexico (I have seen others that actually mention the town and not just Mexico). A quick search with his name and parents also on FamilySearch revealed his baptism record and place of birth as El Encadenado, General Teran, Nuevo Leon, Mexico. This Death certificate provided the clues that ended up with me finding three more generations of Perez.

Let's just keep in mind this is one scenario that may or may not apply to you but what I want you to understand is that Death Certificates are very important and as you can see they can be the key to finding our ancestors. Now that I have beaten that to a pulp, let's see where you can search for Death Certificates.

FamilySearch.org

Family search has death records from all states of the United States. I highly recommend that check them out you can either do a search (https://familysearch.org/search) or browse it's collections (http://mexgenlink.com/iz8e) to find the particular state or county that you need. Many state collections are searchable and others you will need to do manual searches by browsing.

When you do a search if you get a Social Security Death Index result try and browse to see if FamilySearch has the Death Certificates it may be that they are still not searchable and the date provided by the SSI will be your key to locating that record.

Now that you are aware of the importance of death certificates in the next section I will let you know about the Mexico Military Archives.

Historical Archive of the Mexican Military

Did any of your ancestors ever served in the Mexican Military? Imagine if they did what other valuable information you could add to your Genealogy Research. I have often wondered where I could find military documents and I found just the right place. It is the Archivo Historico Militar maintained by SEDENA (Secretaria de la Defensa Nacional).

This archive contains thousands digital documents in regards to the Mexican military from 1821 to 1921, but I have also come to find some documents that are from the Spanish Colonial period.

You can visit the website with his link:

- http://www.archivohistorico2010.sedena.gob.mx/ (http://mexgenlink.com/jp5n)

You can go straight to searching the archives with this link:

- http://www.archivohistorico2010.sedena.gob.mx/busqueda/busqueda.php (http://mexgenlink.com/e4pp)

I know that this military archive will be of great value to you. As for me I found three sets of documents in regards to the founding of Revilla, Mier, and Camargo by Joseph Tienda de Cuervo. All three sets contain a listing of all families of whom many are my ancestors. I even found out that one of them, my 6th great grandfather Miguel Martinez was a Teniente de Capitan.

Unfortunately, when I search for his name nothing comes up.

Some time back I was doing research for a client whom stated that her ancestors was in the Mexican army and had played an important role in a particular battle. I quickly searched for his name but nothing came up using this resource. I searched for the name of the battle and many documents came up. Many of them had his name and signature, many of those documents were written by him.

This proved that if we don't find our ancestors there it is because their names have not been indexed. I discovered that the only thing that has been indexed is the document's title. Try and search for battles that your ancestor might have had fought on.

As promised previously in this book, in the next section you will read about books and the places where you can find them.

Using and Finding books to Find Your Ancestors and expand your Family Tree

In the beginning of this book I mentioned that one of my misconceptions was that I thought that there was no way that I would ever find my ancestors in any books. I also thought that there were no books about them nor any of them had ever written a book.

Let me tell you I was completely wrong. I did find my ancestors in books; I found books written about them, and also books written by them. In this post I will provide you with websites where you can find your ancestors and also provide you with additional ideas of how you can find physical books about them. For physical books you might have to make a short trip to a local library.

How Can I Expand My Family Tree Using Books

Some of the books that you will come across will be ancestor descendant family trees and will contain genealogical data that will take you months to process or enter into your own family tree.

Bellow you will find the resources that I use to find books about my ancestors.

Online Book Repositories to Find Your Mexican Ancestors

Google Books

Google Books (http://books.google.com) - Google Books is a service from Google Inc. that searches the full text of books and magazines that Google has scanned and converted to text using optical character recognition.

In addition these books are stored in Google's digital database and their collection includes rare Genealogy books from Mexico. If you search for an ancestors name and it comes up you will be allowed to read the full page where the name appears.

In some cases you will be allowed to download the book if it is no longer under copy right.

FamilySearch Books

FamilySearch Books (https://books.familysearch.org) - They contain over 60,000 family history books that have been digitized from major U.S. genealogical libraries.

Some books can only be viewed from within a FamilySeach library or center, but I have come across many books that can be downloaded. This resource has helped me grow my Genealogical book library exponentially.

The Internet Archive

Archive.org - The Internet Archive is a nonprofit online digital library with the stated mission of "universal access to all knowledge." It provides the permanent storage of and free public access to nearly three million public domain books.

A book written by one of my ancestors in the 1600's is available for download for free (http://mexgenlink.com/bry6). I have also found other great books about ancestors and also Mexican history to give some context to their lives.

Look At the Citations

Another great way to find books where our ancestors are mentioned is to look at the citations of other researchers. For example; time and time again I have found many books just by looking at the citations of Raul Longoria's Genealogy Database (http://mexgenlink.com/bv9a) (we have many common ancestors). I found his website by just searching Google. Once you get the name of a book you like, you can search for its title using the above mentioned resources or search for it in a library.

Books at Public Libraries and Universities

Have you searched or browsed your public or local University Library's Genealogical Collection. Believe it or not almost all libraries will have a section dedicated to Genealogy. If you ever come across a book that you cannot find online the next best thing is to see if your local library or University has a copy.

For example my local library has thousands of books about genealogy. Many of those books focus on local genealogy and also about Mexico. I have found some great books where my ancestors appear, but let me just warn you these books are for reference only and you cannot check them out. You will actually have to read the books there, unless the library allows you to check a second copy out.

My favorite place of all is my local university (UTPA) since they have a special collection that focuses on South Texas and Northeastern Mexico. They practically have all the rare books that you will ever come across for this area. The books within their collection have provided me with a wealth of information about my ancestors. So far they have over 100 books where at least one of my ancestor's names appears.

Finding Books in a Library near You

If you ever come across a book that you definitely need to check out you can use the following resource to see if your local library or university has a copy of it.

WorldCat

WorldCat.org - WorldCat is a union catalog that itemizes the collections of 72,000 libraries in 170 countries and territories. It is maintained by each individual library.

When you search for a title of a book this search engine will search all the libraries in its database and provide you with the nearest library that has the book available in their collection.

To be clear, there are many more resources than the ones I have mentioned here. I chose these ones since they are the ones that I use and I highly recommend them. These resources and ideas will also provide you with a solid foundation to start searching for books where your ancestors may be written about.

By now you have learned about many resources on how to locate your ancestors but in the next section you will read about the best resource available to you.

Find Your Mexican Ancestors by Losing Your Fear and Reaching out To Others

Yes, that is right lose your fears and reach out to others and you will, I guarantee it, find your ancestors. It took me a few years and my only regret is that I did not start doing it sooner. Other people will be your greatest resource.

Lose Your Fears

What do I mean; I'll be honest for many years I did genealogy research without ever contacting anyone or even talking about my research to anyone. A fear in this case is anything that may be preventing you from contacting researchers that you come across either to network or to inquire if they have a certain ancestor in their database.

Here are some of my personal fears:

- **It is just a hobby; don't want to seem as if I don't know anything.** - This was one of my fears and since genealogy was just a hobby I would fear contacting anyone since I did not want others to think I did not know anything about genealogy. Guess what, kick this fear since it is a learning experience and no one will think you don't know anything and if they do so what? Most people will give you a lending hand and point you in the right

84

direction that is what I do when asked about records or genealogy. I self-thought myself to do genealogy research.

- **I felt intimidated by others with their extensive research.** - When you come across researchers as Crispin Rendon, John Inclan, and Gary Felix you can't help to feel amazed and at the same time think, man my research is nothing compared to theirs. Well let me tell you all three of them are very approachable and nice people to email with. Just remember their Genealogy research at one point was at the same level that yours may be at today. I have had people join my online family tree and tell me that I have too much material and that they may not be able to contribute anything new. I know they are intimidated but I just tell them that it is ok since I am just happy that I am able to share my research with them.

- **What if I share information I should not?** - This was one of my greatest fears; basically I had no idea of what I should share with others and did not feel comfortable sharing family information. The rule of thumb is, do not share living relative's information; I believe that everything else is ok to share. Some people don't share the most recent three generations but it is a personal choice.

These where some of my fears and believe me I had many more. As you read this I know that you probably have already identified some of your own fears or you have already kicked these fears off.

Reaching Out To Others

Let me just assure you that once you stop fearing and start reaching out to others while doing genealogy research you will find the leads that you need to find your elusive Ancestors.

Ways of Reaching Out

- Blogging - This is my favorite way of reaching out. By sharing what I know about my ancestors on my personal blog We Are Cousins (http://www.wearecousins.info) I have meet countless distant cousins.

- Emailing - If you come across your ancestor's on a website send an email to the owner of the website. They will love to hear about you and your common ancestor.

- Forums - These are great, you can just leave inquiries and people will find them. The best one of them in my own opinion is the forum named Mexico Genealogy Forum (http://mexgenlink.com/yw6l) by GenForums.

- Facebook - Is by far the best tool to reach out to others. Just search for Facebook Pages and Groups. I have found countless distant cousins and not to mention even two pictures of my great grandparents. As an example you can check out my Facebook Page for We Are Cousins (https://www.facebook.com/wearecousins) and for Mexican Genealogy (https://www.facebook.com/MexicanGenealogy) for a Facebook Groups check also We Are Cousins (http://mexgenlink.com/xtbj) and the Mexican Genealogy (http://mexgenlink.com/teb4). You can also check out: Locate Your Mexican Ancestors with Facebook Profiles, Pages, and Communities (next chapter).

- Twitter - To be honest with you I have heard that twitter is great but I have only talked to one person about genealogy using twitter. You never know you may be luckier than me.

The above mentioned are just some of the things that I do to reach out and network with other researchers or people that have the same interests as I do.

I highly encourage you to take those first steps to reach out and find your ancestors. Don't forget that making friends is very rewarding. You can start with me; just send me an email introducing yourself to moisesgarza@gmail.com.

You briefly read about facebook in this section but in the next section I will elaborate more on Facebook.

Locate Your Ancestors with Facebook Profiles, Pages, and Communities

Facebook Profiles, Pages, and Communities are a great resource to find your ancestry. Up to this date I am still amazed at the wealth of information that is available on Facebook. If you do not have Facebook you might want to get an account. I know that many of you may not think that Facebook can be a genealogy resource and much less another tool for your genealogical research arsenal. In fact Facebook provides the family historians and the professional genealogist with three different types of resources. These resources are Facebook Profiles, Facebook Pages, and Facebook Communities.

Facebook Profiles

Everyone that has Facebook automatically has a profile page. It is very likely that many of your family members already have Facebook and thus you can search for their profiles. The genealogical information you can usually gather from their profiles is immense. You can find their School name and their graduation year, their date of birth, and in some cases you can find out whom their extended family is if they have tagged other people as their relatives. You can also expect to find information whenever a new family member is born as well as funeral information when one passes away.

Facebook Pages

This is another great resource offered by Facebook. There are many great Facebook pages that focus on various areas within South Texas and Northeastern Mexico Genealogy and History which is my area of research. Here are some examples of pages that you should check out. They offer excellent photos, stories, resources, and family history and also provide a great opportunity for its users and visitors to easily post pictures, stories, current events, history, and even obituaries or death notices for the community.

- Arcabuz Social Club (http://mexgenlink.com/a1on)
- Arqueología del Noreste de México (http://mexgenlink.com/qo39)
- Descendents of Francisco Martinez Guajardo (http://mexgenlink.com/50sw)
- Genealogía y Heráldica de Nuevo León (http://mexgenlink.com/xsvr)
- GuadalajaraDispensas (http://mexgenlink.com/f7ql)
- Hispanic Genealogy Research (http://mexgenlink.com/ryxh)
- Historia de Cadereyta Jiménez, N.L. (http://mexgenlink.com/pvdc)
- Houston Family Search Genealogy Conference (http://mexgenlink.com/3dbj)
- La Palmita Nuevo Leon (http://mexgenlink.com/2206)
- Los Bexareños Genealogical and Historical Society (http://mexgenlink.com/hxwe)
- La Grulla, Texas (http://mexgenlink.com/yd2s)
- Mexican Genealogy (http://mexgenlink.com/6zp1)
- Mexico Genealogy Research (http://mexgenlink.com/46ow)
- Rio Grande Valley Hispanic Genealogical Society (http://mexgenlink.com/70hr)
- Texas Genealogy Research (http://mexgenlink.com/fll6)
- We Are Cousins (http://mexgenlink.com/j5dm)
- Yo Tambien Soy De Arcabuz Tamaulipas (http://mexgenlink.com/zrmi)

Most of the people that run these Facebook pages and Communities have deep roots on those towns and know the surrounding area and the families that live there. Many of them are family historians and genealogists. To follow Facebook pages all you have to do is like the page and you will start seeing their status updates on your wall.

Facebook Communities

Facebook communities are a little different than pages. Some are by invitation only and others are open to the public. I only found the following to be very useful to me. I am sure that their popularity will grow as time passes by. What is great about communities is also the wealth of information they contain and are more interactive than pages. Just like Facebook Pages, they also provide access for its users and visitors to easily post pictures, stories, current events, history, and even obituaries or death notices for the community

- Laredo Genealogical (http://mexgenlink.com/nr6t)
- Mexican Genealogy (http://mexgenlink.com/teb4)
- Technology for Genealogy (http://mexgenlink.com/jon2)
- We Are Cousins (http://mexgenlink.com/xtbj)
- Yo Tambien Soy De Arcabuz (http://mexgenlink.com/7prz)

Be sure to search for communities that may be able to help in your research or area of interest.

Have you searched for your Mexican ancestor's town on Facebook?

You will be surprised, many times someone is already managing a page or community on Facebook about those towns, and many times you will find a friendly face between their members. I use these resources on a daily basis, I have also found pictures of several brothers of my great grandfather, and even very old class pictures of the local school. Not to mention old photos of its people and its buildings thus providing a glimpse to the past.

I have also found distant cousins that I did not know I had, by the way don't be afraid to ask questions and or participate. Since being an active member will be more rewarding.

If you search and you cannot find your ancestors town on Facebook Pages, then create that page and post what you know and I bet that in a short time you will get likeminded people who are also interested and they will post what they know. You can get more details on the following link on how to create a Facebook page: https://www.faceBook.com/business/build

As you can see Facebook is excellent for genealogists and family historians. Also remember there are state websites, and municipality websites so make sure to search for those too. Happy hunting and have fun!

In the next section you will read about another of my recommendations for reaching out. It is about why you should create a blog.

Start Your Own Blog and Share Your Mexican Genealogy

Have you ever wanted to publish or share your stories, genealogical information, and family history with others? If you have thought about this and have no idea how to do it just keep on reading. I will let you know why creating a blog is perfect for this.

What is a Blog

Wikipedia describes it as - A blog (a contraction of the words web log) is a discussion or informational site published on the World Wide Web and consisting of discrete entries ("posts") typically displayed in reverse chronological order (the most recent post appears first).

An example:

- www.wearecousins.info - My own personal blog about South Texas and Northeastern Mexico where I document resources and my own family genealogy.

Why Create a Blog

A blog is the perfect platform to share genealogical information, photos and family history about your family. It is ideal to share all this information with others. A blog is also ideal since you can only share what you want and at your own pace. You can share as often as you want.

Also the benefits of a blog are immense; you will meet distant cousins and also help you increase your level of documentation when it comes to your own ancestors. It is also a perfect networking tool.

Besides it is a platform that is used by millions of Bloggers worldwide.

What to Share?

I know that at the beginning this can be intimidating and have no idea of what you should or should not share. I started by only sharing family group information and then to posting resources that would help others in their research. Finally, I have shared copies of original documents with their transcription, family photos, and family stories.

I have also run into some skeletons and sensitive information and have opted to keep these private in order to avoid needless trouble with relatives. My main rule is that I ask myself "Would my mother be embarrassed to read my blog? If the answer is yes, don't share it.

I am Interested, How do I Start a Blog?

What I recommend that you do is start with a free service to test it out. Once you determine that you are in for the long run, you can use a paid option but not necessary as I will later explain.

Free Blog Platforms

I will only talk about two of them since they are the ones that I have used can really recommend with confidence.

- Blogger.com - Is owned by Google and is easier to use with a straight forward interface. This is the one where WeAreCousins (http://www.wearecousins.info) (my personal blog) started. Perfect for starters and advanced users. It also lets you use your own domain name.

- Wordpress.com - Wordpress is just a bit harder to use but it might provide you with additional features that Blogger won't. It also has limited templates to change look and feel of website.

Self-Hosting Your Own Blog

If what you want is to be able to have more flexibility and have your blog work harder for you then you might want to host your own blog. Wordpress.org is perfect for this and I highly recommend it since that is what I use for all my websites and also my own blog.

- Wordpress.org - Allows you to download the software that is made and used by wordpress.com but this is for more advanced users since you will need a domain name, hosting space, and be able to upload the Wordpress installation files. This option provides thousands of templates and many paid templates are also available.

If you want to go this route and need help setting everything out check out bytemunchers.com for their services.

Affiliates of Mexican Genealogy

- Bluehost.com - Is what I use to host my websites, they are perfect to host your own blog since they can register your domain name, host your blog, and they provide a one click install for Wordpress. You can set up a blog in less than five minutes.

- <u>Godaddy.com</u> - This is what I use to host my domain names, they also provide hosting services but you need to use an FTP Tool to upload Wordpress.

I hope that you found this section useful and that it also guides you on the right path to creating your own blog to share your genealogical information. Remember that the more blogs out there about Mexican ancestors the better we all are.

Even if you never start your own family blog, please do follow the recommendation that I give you in the next section since it is vital to finding your ancestors.

Always Keep Learning

Always keep on learning bout Mexican Genealogy resources that are out there and also about methods that you can apply to your own research. Learning is essential to finding our ancestors. You never know when you will come across a clue or an idea/method that will help you bring down your brick walls.

The following are places that I use to find resources and find materials to keep on learning.

- FamilySearch Mexico Wiki (http://mexgenlink.com/6xly) - A community website whose main purpose is to help people throughout the world learn how to find their ancestors. Here you can learn how to find, use, and analyze Mexican records of genealogical value. Its content is targeted to beginners, intermediate, and expert researchers.

- Google.com - Google is your best tool to learn about Mexican Genealogy since it is the biggest gateway to the internet and has billions of pages indexed and many great resources can be found there.

- MexicanGenealogy.info - If you have Mexican Ancestry this is the best place to start your Mexican Genealogy research and is an excellent resource to anyone doing Genealogy Research in Mexico. Also get help getting started in Mexican Genealogy.

- Facebook.com - As previously mentioned Facebook has many groups dedicated to Genealogy, family history, and many regional pages. Following them is essential; you never know what you might learn.

- WorldCat.org - You can use it to find books about Genealogy and also many books about how to get started in genealogy. This website will help you locate the material you want in a library near you.

- Geneabloggers.com - Contains a huge listing of Genealogy blogs, I follow many of them to get ideas of how other people do research and I always learn about new resources or ideas on how to search for my ancestors. I highly recommend that you find some active blogs, posting daily or weekly, and follow them with an rss reader.

Remember that Genealogy is something that you learn how to do and also you need to keep up to date with advances in this field. It does not matter if you are a professional or a beginner you have to keep on learning.

I know that you are on the right path since just by reading this book you already have ample knowledge and a solid foundation to get you on the right track on finding you Mexican roots.

To get you started in expanding your knowledge in the next section I have provided an excellent resource for you.

Major Genealogical Record Sources in Mexico

As I just mentioned "Always Keep Learning" and to get you started I have included this great resource.

Download and read this book "Major Genealogical Record Sources in Mexico" it is an excellent resource to help you in your Genealogical Research and after you read it you will have the same opinion about it. It is a small 22 page book available at familysearch.org. This book was written by the Church of Jesus Christ of Latter-day Saints Genealogical Department back in 1970 but the material covered is as relevant today as it was back then.

The four major goals of this book are to:

- Identify types of records that exist that will aid in the identification of ancestors.

- Identify periods of time that the existing records cover.

- Identify what genealogical information appears in the existing records.

- Identify the availability of existing records for searching.

Download book here:

http://mexgenlink.com/2ldv

This book has already helped me to identify several books were possible ancestors may be listed. I know that it will also help you out. Even if you do not have the time to check it out today or read it I recommend that you download it.

In the following section I will also provide you with an excellent resource to Mexican Genealogical Research by states.

The Mexican Genealogy Research Online by State Project

The key to finding your Mexican Ancestors and Ancestry is access to resources. In this time and age many of these resources are popping up online and providing access to other wise hard to get collections. When I started mexicangenalogy.info one of my original intentions was to eventually create a post for each Mexican state and try/attempt to list all the available resources that are online for that particular state. I know that this will be of great interest and also of great help you.

My intention was to post every state here with its direct link but I decided to just provide you with the link to the Projects Main page: http://mexicangenealogy.info/research/by-state/

I will eventually put all of these state pages together into a book titled "Online Mexican Genealogy Resources by State". Be on the lookout for it at mexicangenalogybooks.com.

Conclusion

After reading this book you should now have a solid foundation to start the very rewarding task of building your own family tree and of finding your ancestors and their stories. I don't have much to say to you as parting words, but I do want to make you aware that you are not alone and that you can join the community at Facebook. There are many other people just like you and me that are willing to help each other and also learn from each other.

If you are researching family from South Texas, Tamaulipas, Nuevo Leon, and Coahuila I highly recommend that you join the Facebook group that I created specifically for this area.

Here is the link: https://www.facebook.com/groups/wacgroup/

If you are researching ancestors from other Mexican States then I recommend that you join our Mexican genealogy group also on Facebook.

Here is the link:
https://www.facebook.com/groups/mexicangenealogy/

Don't forget to follow us at:

Mexican Genealogy Academy

If interested in learning more about Mexican Genealogy you can join our Academy at http://mexicangenealogyacademy.com/

You will get access to all my eBooks, access to many other eBooks, access to our Video Library, and best of all you can get one on one help with any questions that you may have.

List of all Resources Mentioned in This Guide

Here are all the resources that I mention in this guide for easy access. That way you don't have to browse through the whole book to try and find the resource that you need.

Baptisms

- Mexico, Baptisms, 1560-1950 (http://mexgenlink.com/kqpg) – FamilySearch's searchable database of Mexican Catholic Baptisms

Blog Platforms

- Blogger.com - Is a blog-publishing service that allows private or multi-user blogs with time-stamped entries.
- Wordpress.com - Start a WordPress blog or create a free website in minutes
- Wordpress.org - A semantic personal publishing platform with a focus on aesthetics, web standards, and usability.

Books

- Borderlands Book Store (http://www.borderlandsbooks.com) - Promotes awareness about the history of the Spanish and Portuguese Empires, Mexico and Mexican Republic.
- Index to the Marriage Investigations of the Diocese of Guadalajara 1653 - 1750 (http://mexgenlink.com/1mnt) – Books with synopsis of documents in the Diocese of Guadalajara.
- Los Marroquin de el Valle de Santiago del Guaxuco (http://mexgenlink.com/pxxz) – Books about the Marroquin.
- Historia de Nuevo Leon con Noticias de Coahuila, Tejas, Nuevo Mexico (http://mexgenlink.com/bry6) - Book
- WorldCat.org - Find what you want in a library near you with WorldCat, a global catalog of library collections.

Border Crossings

- Border Crossings: From Mexico to U.S., 1895-1964 (http://mexgenlink.com/cjks) - This database contains an index of aliens and some citizens crossing into the U.S. from Mexico via various ports of entry along the U.S.-Mexican border between 1895 and 1964.
- Crossing the Frontera (http://mexgenlink.com/ym23)- This class will give you a little background information about these records and their content.
- National Archives (http://mexgenlink.com/p9kv) – Information about Mexican Border Crossing Records.
- United States, Border Crossings from Mexico to United States, 1903-1957 (http://mexgenlink.com/wy9d)- Index to records of aliens and citizens crossing into the United States of America from Mexico via various ports of entry along the U.S.-Mexican border between 1903 and 1957.

Catholic Church Record Images

- Catholic Church Records (http://mexgenlink.com/0cne) - List of all Mexican Church Records available at FamilySearch.org.

Citing Sources

- APA Style (http://mexgenlink.com/q2xr) - APA citation style refers to the rules and conventions established by the American Psychological Association for documenting sources used in a research paper.
- MLA Style (http://mexgenlink.com/6trq)- The Modern Language Association (MLA) establishes values for acknowledging sources used in a research paper.

Civil Registration Record Images

- Mexican Civil Registry Records (http://mexgenlink.com/rpr9) – List of all Mexican Civil Registry Records available at FamilySearch.org.

Deaths

- Mexico, Deaths, 1680-1940 (http://mexgenlink.com/uozh) - Index to selected Catholic Church death records from various localities in Mexico

eBooks

- Google Books (http://books.google.com) - Search and preview millions of books from libraries and publishers worldwide

- FamilySearch Books (https://books.familysearch.org) – Collection of 100000 genealogical eBooks, non-copyrighted books are available for viewing and download.
- Archive.org - The Internet Archive Text Archive contains a wide range of historical texts and some genealogy texts.

Facebook Communities

- Laredo Genealogical (http://mexgenlink.com/nr6t) – Facebook Page focusing on the Genealogy of Laredo.
- Mexican Genealogy (http://mexgenlink.com/teb4)
- Technology for Genealogy (http://mexgenlink.com/jon2) - Facebook Group where any type of technology used for genealogy is discussed.
- We Are Cousins (http://mexgenlink.com/xtbj)
- Yo tambien soy de Arcabuz (http://mexgenlink.com/7prz) – Facebook Group focusing on the small town of Arcabuz, Tamaulipas, Mexico.

Facebook Pages

- Arcabuz Social Club (http://mexgenlink.com/a1on) – Facebook Page of the Arcabuz Social Club, You can find old photos and also obituary notices from people of this town.
- Arqueología del Noreste de México (http://mexgenlink.com/qo39) – Page focusing on archeology of Tamaulipas.
- Descendents of Francisco Martinez Guajardo (http://mexgenlink.com/50sw) – Page where the descendants of Francisco Martinez Guajardo post their new findings about their ancestors.
- Genealogía y Heráldica de Nuevo León – Page focusing on the Genealogy and History of Nuevo Leon, Mexico.
- Genealogia y Historia de Mexico (http://mexgenlink.com/xsvr) – Page focusing on the Genealogy and history of Mexico

- GuadalajaraDispensas (http://mexgenlink.com/f7ql) – Contains Indexes of almost all years of the Dispensas found in diocese of Guadalajara which used to cover most of Mexico on its early years.
- Hispanic Genealogy Research (http://mexgenlink.com/ryxh) – Provides tips about genealogy and information about conferences.
- Historia de Cadereyta Jiménez, N.L. (http://mexgenlink.com/pvdc) – Page focusing only on the history of Cadereyta Jimenez but I have also found great genealogy information about my ancestors.
- Houston Family Search Genealogy Conference (http://mexgenlink.com/3dbj) – Provides information about the Houston Family Search Conference.
- La Palmita Nuevo Leon (http://mexgenlink.com/2206) – Page focusing on the History and Genealogy of this small town.
- Los Bexareños Genealogical and Historical Society (http://mexgenlink.com/hxwe) – Get updates about their meetings and much more.
- La Grulla, Texas (http://mexgenlink.com/yd2s) – Page focusing on current events and history about La Grulla, Texas. Obituaries posted also form time to time.
- Mexican Genealogy (http://mexgenlink.com/6zp1) – Page where all posts of mexicangeenalogy.info are posted and its purpose if to help anyone with their Mexican Genealogy Research.
- Mexico Genealogy Research (http://mexgenlink.com/46ow) – Page focusing on resources to help you find your Mexican Ancestors.
- Rio Grande Valley Hispanic Genealogical Society (http://mexgenlink.com/70hr) – Page for the RGVHGS.
- Texas Genealogy Research (http://mexgenlink.com/fll6) – Page focusing on Texas Genealogy Research.
- We Are Cousins (http://mexgenlink.com/j5dm) – Page focusing on South Texas and Northeastern Mexico Genealogy.

- Yo Tambien Soy De Arcabuz Tamaulipas
  (http://mexgenlink.com/zrmi) – Page focusing on this small
  town's history and genealogy.

Facebook Page Creation

- https://www.faceBook.com/business/build - Information on
  how to create your own Facebook Page.

Genealogy Websites

- ancestry.com – Contains various collections about Mexico.
- www.familysearch.org – If you could only use one website
  for your Genealogy research this will be it. They have
  hundreds of collections pertaining to Mexico.
- geni.com – You can create an online tree with them or just
  search for your ancestors to connect with other researchers.
- google.com – The heart of genealogy research, here you can
  find almost anything. If it is in the web and Google has
  crawled it you will find it.
- Guadalajara Dispensas
  (http://www.guadalajaradispensas.com) – Contains indexes
  to almost all the microfilms from the diocese of Gudalajara,
  Mexico.
- mexicangenealogy.info – Blog focusing on Mexican
  Genealogy tips and resources.
- Mexico Genealogy Forum (http://mexgenlink.com/yw6l) –
  Forum where you will find thousands of Mexican Genealogy
  Inquiries.
- myheritage.com – Website where you can download free
  genealogy software and also search for your ancestors to
  connect with other researchers.

- raullongoria.net – Personal website of Raul Longoria whom has been doing genealogy research for many years.
- Raul Longoria's Genealogy Database (http://mexgenlink.com/bv9a) - Contains a database of people from South Texas and Northeastern Mexico.
- SAGA (http://www.sagacorpuschristi.com) – Spanish American Genealogical Association, you can find books of indexes to many Mexican towns.
- wearecousins.info - Blog focusing on South Texas and Northeastern Mexico Genealogy tips and resources.
- wikytree.com – You can create your own family tree or search for your ancestors.
- Wikipidia.org - Contains biographies and history about many people and places from Mexico.

Guides to Put PDF on Devises

- How to add PDF files to read in iBooks on your iPad, iPod Touch or iPhone (http://mexgenlink.com/bsw5)
- How to Read PDF on Android Phones & Tablets? (http://mexgenlink.com/g9h2)

File Back Up

- DropBox.com – Get up to 2 free gigabytes.
- Box.com - Get up to 2 free gigabytes.

Forms and Charts

- Family Group Sheet Form (http://mexgenlink.com/egxd) – PDF Document

- Five Generation Ancestor Chart
  (http://mexgenlink.com/z5m7) - PDF Document
- Relationship Chart (http://mexgenlink.com/mtks) - PDF
  Document

Marriages

- Mexico, Marriages, 1570-1950
  (http://mexgenlink.com/wnyh) - Index to selected Catholic
  Church marriage records from various localities in Mexico.

Mexico 1930 Census

- Ancestry – 1930 Mexico National Census
  (http://mexgenlink.com/1tl4)
- FamilySearch – Mexico Census, 1930
  (http://mexgenlink.com/exg0)
- FamilySearch Wiki – Mexico 1930 Census Information
  (http://mexgenlink.com/14uc)

Search Engines

- FamilySearch's Searching Guide
  (http://mexgenlink.com/uzo9) – Guide on how to conduct
  internet searches.
- Google Search (https://www.google.com) – Best search
  engine out there.
- Google Search Operators (http://mexgenlink.com/tzo5) –
  Special search techniques that can help you narrow your
  searches.
- randymajors.com – Great genealogy search engine that uses
  Google as its backbone.

Searchable State Civil Registry Databases:

- Coahuila Civil Registry Births (http://mexgenlink.com/cq9w)
- Coahuila Civil Registry Deaths (http://mexgenlink.com/do4j)
- Coahuila Civil Registry Divorces
  (http://mexgenlink.com/pa3q)
- Coahuila Civil Registry Marriages
  (http://mexgenlink.com/wm4p)
- Colima Civil Registry Births (http://mexgenlink.com/pa4i)
- Colima Civil Registry Deaths (http://mexgenlink.com/vnuo)
- Colima Civil Registry Divorces
  (http://mexgenlink.com/ilbw)
- Colima Civil Registry Marriages
  (http://mexgenlink.com/140e)
- Guerrero Civil Registry Births (http://mexgenlink.com/lzi8)
- Guerrero Civil Registry Marriages
  (http://mexgenlink.com/g048)
- Guerrero Civil Registry Deaths (http://mexgenlink.com/tezi)
- Tamaulipas Civil Registry Births
  (http://mexgenlink.com/4iao)
- Tamaulipas Civil Registry Marriages
  (http://mexgenlink.com/n532)

Software

- Family Tree Maker (http://familytreemaker.com) – Paid
  software to enter all your family's information.
- Family Tree Builder (http://mexgenlink.com/qz1i) – Free
  software to enter all your family's information.
- Genscriber (http://mexgenlink.com/ak5h) - GenScriber is a
  transcription editor for census records, church records, birth,
  marriage, baptisms, burials, index records etc.
- Transcript 2.3 (http://mexgenlink.com/korr) - A program
  designed to help you to transcribe the text on digital images
  of documents.

Transcribing

- <u>English Tutorial</u> (http://mexgenlink.com/oqxt) – Tutorial on how to transcribe documents.
- <u>Genscriber</u> (http://mexgenlink.com/ak5h) - GenScriber is a transcription editor for census records, church records, birth, marriage, baptisms, burials, index records etc.
- <u>Spanish Tutorial</u> (http://mexgenlink.com/ninc) - Tutorial on how to transcribe documents.
- <u>Spanish Genealogical Word List</u> (http://mexgenlink.com/h1eh) - Words that you are likely to find in genealogical sources translated into English.
- <u>Spanish Name Abbreviations</u> (http://mexgenlink.com/jnic) – Most common abbreviations of Mexican Names.
- <u>Transcription Rules & Techniques</u> (http://mexgenlink.com/ahyo) – Short article describing Transcriptions.
- <u>Transcript 2.3</u> (http://mexgenlink.com/korr) - A program designed to help you to transcribe the text on digital images of documents.

Web Hosting

- <u>Bluehost.com</u> – Web hosting provider in case that you are looking to start your own genealogy website or blog.
- <u>Godaddy.com</u> - Web hosting provider in case that you are looking to start your own genealogy website or blog.

22102248R00072

Made in the USA
Columbia, SC
23 July 2018